RoSA is a small registered charity based in Rugby, Warwickshire, that provides counselling and support for women, men and young people who have experienced rape or sexual abuse at any time in their lives. RoSA trains and supervises volunteers to provide a specialist support service for survivors and also works to raise awareness of the needs and issues of male and female survivors.

Everyone at RoSA is well aware that many survivors are not able to access the kind of support that they need, and often feel isolated and alone in their experiences. The Survivors Guide to Recovery from Rape and Sexual Abuse is our attempt to reach out to survivors everywhere, to help them take control of their lives again, and to help them feel that they are not alone.

All funds received from the sale of The Survivors Guide will be used to support our voluntary service and to fund further editions.

We will be very pleased to receive your comments if you wish to contact us, but callers should remember that RoSA is a small service, run entirely by volunteers, and may not be able to respond immediately. There is a list of contact numbers for support services and helplines in the UK in Chapter 12.

Our website survivor.guide.co.uk includes information, leading articles, up-to-date research and additional materials. There is also a bulletin board for visitors to leave their comments.

RoSA,
PO Box 151, Rugby. CV21 3WR
www.survivorguide.co.uk

The Survivor's Guide

To Recovery from Rape and Sexual Abuse

by

Robert Kelly and Fay Maxted

Illustrated by

Elizabeth Campbell

Published by Rugby RoSA

© RoSA 2005

By Robert Kelly and Fay Maxted

Edited by: George Ttoouli

Designed and typeset by: Leigh Hunt

Illustrations: Elizabeth Campbell

Additional illustrations: Fay Maxted

First Published in Great Britain by:
RoSA, PO Box 151, Rugby. CV21 3WR
www.survivorguide.co.uk

ISBN:
0-9551037-0-3
978-0-9551037-0-4

Printed and bound in Great Britain by:
Graphic Solutions
Coventry
CV3 4LJ

DEDICATION

There are millions of survivors who have no opportunity to speak. They have no possibility of making their voice heard. Sometimes, as a result of what has happened, they are unable to live effective lives.

This book is dedicated to all the millions of survivors across the world.
Here they have an opportunity to be given encouragement.

Survivors unite around the world

CONTENTS

FOREWORD #1

In a legal career of over 25 years, latterly as a prosecutor, I have dealt with many people who have abused others and those who have been abused. For victims of abuse, disclosure can be the first step to becoming a survivor whether it results in legal proceedings or not. For many, it will be the first time that they fully appreciate that they are not the only person who has suffered in this way, breaking down isolation that can be such a barrier to recovery. For all that, the law is a blunt instrument for such a complex issue and one in which until recently, the main focus was on the abuser, with witnesses playing only a subservient role.

Robert Kelly and Fay Maxted have created a book that puts those who feel they have no power on centre stage. Here is a means whereby they can take back some control of their lives, whether what happened to them was years ago or yesterday. Its straight forward language and practical approach makes it widely accessible, and it holds out a valuable hand to hold, even if there is no one else to turn to.

As a Soroptimist, I am proud that members in Rugby have played a large part in making this book happen. Their close association with RoSA has helped create a lasting resource in an area that is one of the last taboos in our society.

Soroptimists have never been afraid to support the most vulnerable or champion a difficult cause, and this book will be a fine testament to their values as well as the skill of the authors and the courage of the survivors who have contributed to it.

Janet Garnons-Williams
Prosecution Team Leader, Crown Prosecution Service Kent
Federation President, Soroptimist International of Great Britain
and Ireland 2004-5

FOREWORD #2

As a lawyer working in the field of child protection, I read on an almost daily basis of children who have suffered sexual abuse, who have been the victims of or witnessed domestic violence or who have endured emotional or physical neglect. Often, psychological assessments of such children's carers reveal that they themselves have experienced some kind of abuse or trauma in the past. Such carers may need to deal with those experiences before they will be able to look after and protect children.

As I read through this guide to recovery from rape and sexual abuse, I found many concepts that I recognised from my work. The feelings of isolation, helplessness and guilt, coupled with low self-esteem, experienced by survivors of abuse, were all familiar to me.

The guide makes it clear that, for counselling to be effective, a survivor of abuse has to be ready to deal with the issues that it will raise. Having a child taken away is often enough to spur a parent into facing his or her own demons from the past. Unfortunately, waiting lists for counselling can be lengthy and the therapy itself can take a long time. Children cannot always wait for their parents to overcome their own problems.

A book such as this can help survivors of abuse in so many ways. It may give comfort and hope to those survivors who are not yet able to seek formal counselling, it can 'fill in the gap' while a survivor waits for that first appointment with a counsellor and it can be on the shelf, waiting to be read when times get tough during counselling.

Whether you read this guide to help yourself or to help others, you have my very best wishes.

Carol Strongman
Barrister
President, Midland Arden Region of Soroptimist International
2004-5

FOREWORD #3

Before the start of my year as President of Soroptimist International of Rugby I chose RoSA as both our charity and our Programme Action focus. I explained that I did not want simply to raise money and would like the Club to get involved in a project that would have a lasting impact – could they possibly think of anything? Fay mentioned that she and Robert were writing a book, and so that became the Club project – and one which we hope will have a very lasting impact!

The past year has been hard work, in raising the money for publishing the book and to produce a CD that has been distributed to every Soroptimist Club in the UK. It has also been a time of celebration that so many talented people have been prepared to give their time and skills for the benefit of the project, and at no cost. There have also been some very moving times, particularly in reading the case studies in the book and hearing the stories of other survivors. I hope that the end result will help others during an extremely difficult period of their lives.

I really must thank all Soroptimists, friends and their relations who have given so generously and have helped in so many ways. In particular I wish to thank Hannah Reynolds of Zarr Internet Services who has set up a RoSA website completely free of charge, and Becky Hutson of Sparks PR who has publicised the project and the book – without them both we would not be where we are now where we are now.

We hope that this book will help you in your quest for peace, and that the proceeds raised will help ROSA to print more books and will also provide much needed revenue to help them to carry on their fantastic and, sadly, very necessary job.

With best wishes

Leigh Hunt
President, Soroptimist International of Rugby 2004-5

ACKNOWLEDGEMENTS

The authors would like to thank Leigh Hunt for her untiring work and ceaseless belief in this book. With her determination our work has grown and been strengthened. We thank the Soroptimist International of Rugby without whose support we would not have been able to publish this book.

We are indebted to George Ttooulie for his patience as editor. George has given his time and attention beyond the call of duty.

Special thanks are due to Elizabeth Campbell for her thought-provoking illustrations. We would also like to thank Hannah Reynolds of Zarr Internet Services for her help with the website, and Becky Hutson from Sparks PR who helped with the publicity.

Thanks to Kris Connolly for his support. We thank David O'Connell, Chair of Rugby RoSA, for his belief that this project was worthwhile, and all those survivors and supporters who gave their time to read and give constructive criticism during the writing of this book. Thanks to Keiron Knights for his poem and letter.

Thanks to all the survivors who shared their experiences and healing with us.

CHAPTER 1

HOW TO USE THIS BOOK

INTRODUCTION

This is a guide for survivors of rape and sexual abuse. It is a first step for anyone who wants to look at the impact sexual abuse has had in their lives. It can help you to begin your journey towards healing.

Many survivors cannot make great progress in their lives. It is hoped that, with the right support, you will be able not only to survive, but also to thrive and be successful in your life.

You are not alone in your experiences. Hopefully you will feel able to take positive steps towards healing. However, you have to feel ready to take these steps and you must proceed in your own time. You may just want to go slowly at first and then come back to the rest later on. There is no straightforward route to healing.

This is a difficult journey, and you will reach deep inside of yourself and by the end of it use much emotional energy as you work through the topics. Do not fear. We will stay with you every step of the way.

We want you to know that there are individuals who have been there and experienced great anguish, but wish to share their journey on the road to healing and living fulfilling lives.

As far as we know, there did not exist a book that dealt with this subject matter in this particular way. There are many textbooks

How to use this book

written for counsellors or health professionals, with many theories of why and how rape and sexual abuse happens and what the impact can be on an individual.

What we are interested in is how you can find ways to cope with the impact abuse may have had on your life, on a day-to-day basis. Even more than that, for you to find a way to move through coping to living an inspired life.

We wanted a friendly book, which invited the reader to participate in its ideas. The aim is to help survivors to honour themselves: for you to trust your own powers of recovery and to respect the many ways you have learned to survive.

You should be able to find something helpful for you here no matter what stage you are at in your recovery.

Always, we want to remind you – be kind to yourself

This book is for anyone who is a survivor of rape or sexual abuse. You may be male or female or transgender. You may have been young or old when you experienced rape or sexual abuse. We are offering you a survival guide for now and the future.

You may be reading this book before you have had the opportunity to speak to anyone else about your experiences. The aim, then, would be for you to start looking at the positive steps towards recovery that can encourage you.

You may be a partner or friend of someone who has experienced trauma. In this case, you will find information and insight to help and encourage you in supporting them.

Whatever has brought you to this book, go well on your journey
and take our good wishes with you

GETTING THE MOST FROM THIS BOOK

The key to getting the most from this book is in understanding how the experience of trauma affects someone. Rape and sexual abuse create a deep wound within the core of someone's being. The pain and hurt is felt at a level that bypasses the rational thinking part of the mind.

At the core of our personalities we have the part of ourselves that still feels like a child. This is often called our 'inner child'. It is the part of our personalities that is still in touch with the intense emotions we experienced as children, both joyful and fearful. It is the spontaneous and unrestricted part of our personality that reacts to the world with feelings and emotions that have all the intensity and energy of a two-year-old child.

Trauma wounds our inner child, creating feelings and thoughts about ourselves that are rooted in our inner child's way of reacting to the world. That is, our reactions to trauma come from a time when, if something bad happened, the feelings we experienced were fear and shame.

You may have said yourself that you understand, rationally, that you are not to blame for being abused or raped, but the feelings inside your heart are still of guilt and shame. This is because it is your inner child that is wounded and it has not yet been able to connect with, or emotionally understand, your rational thoughts.

What this means is that any healing journey has to work in two ways:

1. It has to inform and build your understanding and self-awareness of the possible impact of trauma on your life.
2. And it has to link with your inner child; to develop and nurture new feelings and emotional responses in the way you react to your understanding of traumatic experiences.

This book is a catalyst to get you on the road towards healing. It has been written with extensive survivor input and consultation. We have used a variety of information sections, writing and journal space, ideas for creative ways of expressing feelings, and reminders for self-nurturing and encouragement.

We have also included three stories from survivors who have suffered sexual abuse at different times in their lives. Many survivors feel isolated and alone and feel as though their experiences have made them different to everyone else in society. We have used the stories to illustrate the different experiences survivors can have and to demonstrate how recovery can happen.

The stories are based on real experiences that are true to life. We have used these stories to demonstrate what the impact of rape and sexual abuse can be and to show how survivors learn to cope with their experiences.

To get the most from this book you might want to:

➢ Plan how you will work with this book. Planning how you are going to get the most from this book will be the first way of demonstrating to yourself your own power to achieve. The section on 'Planning how to use this book' (page 10) has ideas to help you decide what you need to do to help yourself get the most out of your time

➢ Think about what's said in the book – how does it apply to you in your own particular situation?

➢ Think about how you could put into practice any of the ideas suggested – there is a lot of practical advice on support

➢ Keep a diary of your healing journey – you can use this book to keep your notes and sketches. You will be able to look back over your notes and see how far you have come, along the road of healing

➢ If you absolutely cannot keep a diary on paper, then keep a journal in your mind. This is necessary because it will let you acknowledge to yourself where you have come from and where you are going to

➤ Try out the self-care ideas – they're easily identified by the Activity symbol

They are a vital part of reclaiming your life and sense of self-esteem through emotionally supporting your inner child

➤ The information throughout this book may help you to identify some of the real difficulties that prevent you from feeling in control of your life. Then you can identify what you might need to do or change, to make things better

➤ You can also use the book to help explain to someone what is happening to you on the road to healing

➤ You can choose to focus on specific topics, or use it as a whole course for an individual recovery programme. You can use the book on its own, or preferably share it with a supporter

➤ We end with your vision of what you would like to achieve for yourself

Help is at Hand

First of all, we want to remind you that you may have to take care. There is no substitute for human contact. Many survivors feel alienated and alone. Reading this might bring up issues that you will find hard to deal with. Even though you have people around you, it may be that you still feel isolated and without support. In this case, the suggestions for caring for yourself are even more important.

We hope that, if you want to explore your problems, you will be able to find someone to talk to. There are organisations out there that can help. A list of support organisations, helplines and websites can be found at the back of this book (page 323).

While we do provide lots of suggestions for self-help, we recommend that, in order to get the maximum benefit from the book, you do seek out a supporter, counsellor, therapist or support organisation.

INNER WISDOM

You might be thinking, 'What difference will writing about things make? You can't change the past or alter what's happened.'

That's true enough. But, what you can change and alter is how you are being affected now, what is happening for you today, what you make of today and how you feel today - and that's what really matters.

There's no doubt, and lots of research to show this, that the effects of trauma can be devastating on someone's life, relationships and achievements.

It may take many years for someone to recognise how their lives have been affected by trauma, but they are often aware at some level that something just isn't working in their lives.

It seems like, no matter how hard they try, things just don't work out as they want them to. If they are asked, they may say things like, 'I can't trust anyone', or 'I can't keep my temper'.

Later on we look at this more, but first we wanted to encourage you to get in touch with your gut feelings – the little voice inside you that's connected to your instincts and conscience; that tells you what needs to be different for you to feel better.

When we thought of this little voice, we could only call it our inner wisdom.

Some people might not value their inner wisdom. We have used pictures of wizards to represent the inner knowledge that we all have but sometimes refuse to recognise. The wizards encouraged us to acknowledge some of the deep inner wisdom we have inside ourselves that we will need to draw on in order to succeed.

So, let's introduce you to our Wizards. One represents the voice of your inner child who is connected to your instinctive reactions and feelings – the little voice that tells you when something just doesn't feel right.

The other is the voice of experience and wisdom gained through life experience.

Whenever they appear they will help to guide you in developing your own inner wisdom.

They will hopefully inspire you at many different stages on your personal journey to develop your own inner personality, your inner strength, to become who you need to be, in order to be the person that you want to be.

You will have to give yourself permission to be successful. They will open the door to encourage you. It might be that you have never been encouraged or supported at any point in your life. You get that opportunity here.

Many survivors have difficulty in trusting their own inner wisdom, so we are using the Wizards to remind you to listen to your own instinctive reactions and thoughts about what is happening in your life and to respect your own inner wisdom.

PLANNING TO WORK WITH THIS BOOK

You have the right to give yourself the chance to get your life back on track and you deserve to make the most of the time you spend getting there. If you plan how you will use this time and effort, you will be giving yourself the best chance you can to get the most benefit.

First, we recommend that you find a safe, comfortable space where you can read undisturbed. We would suggest you do not read or work through any exercises at night time. Decide to give yourself the time and encouragement to read and think about the contents, including time after reading to wind down and relax. Have plenty of breaks for drinks or to go for a walk if the going gets tough.

Your plan doesn't have to be set in stone. It can be as simple or involved as you like. You may just decide to write or draw something every time there is a journal space in the book. You might want to make your own mood box and recreate your story and history through the objects you choose to include. You might want to start your own diary or journal and write about your feelings every day. Whatever you choose, make your plan work for you.

If you know you are someone who loses enthusiasm after a short time, then you could include this knowledge in your plan. Skip to other sections further on in the book to maintain interest, or decide to have a break from working on the book for a few weeks so you can come back to it afresh. If you are someone who needs encouragement, then decide how you can reward yourself as you work through the stages in the book.

KEEPING A JOURNAL

Keeping a Journal is part of the healing process

You can use this book to help you keep a journal. We have left spaces for you to make notes, write or draw if you would like to. If you feel uncomfortable carrying the book round with you, then you can cover it to protect your privacy.

It might be a long time since you kept a diary, but making a few notes every day can help you to keep perspective and focus your thoughts.

The reason that we suggest you keep a journal is because it can support the healing process.

It will help you in:

- ➤ Identifying emotions
- ➤ Expressing feelings
- ➤ Getting your thoughts clear
- ➤ Making memories real
- ➤ Keeping a record of your healing journey

You might want to include:

- ➤ How you feel at the time you are writing
- ➤ What you have discovered about yourself
- ➤ What has happened to you in the past and in the present
- ➤ How you want things to change

How to use this book

You'll also find that in the months to come, you will be able to look back through your journal and trace the path you have come along on your way to recovery and healing – the times when you felt better, the times when things seemed to be just as bad, and the times when you recovered from setbacks.

Don't feel that you can only write. You can use words but you can also use pictures. It is not about how good an artist you are. What matters is what the drawing means to you. You could cut out pictures from magazines. You could find pictures that express how you are feeling. Or you could look for poems that help express how you feel.

Some people feel they can write poems about their experiences. We have included some survivor poems elsewhere.

Or you might want to make a collage. Some people can gather objects that seem to capture how you are feeling. You can keep them in a box or use them to make a collage.

What will your journal look like?

- ➢ You might like to get a scrap book
- ➢ Or you might prefer a book with lines to write on
- ➢ Or there are books with black pages
- ➢ You might prefer a diary
- ➢ Or you might simply use a folder to keep your papers in
- ➢ You might prefer a notebook
- ➢ You might like to create something with a beautiful decorated cover

KEEPING A MOOD BOX

Keeping a Mood Box as a step towards healing

If you are the kind of person who doesn't like writing, you could make up a mood box as well as, or instead of, any notes you keep in your journal.

In TV makeover programmes, they ask clients to create a mood board of the colours, textures and ideas they would like to have for a room or garden makeover. Who says you can't do the same for yourself, as a way of recording how you feel as you go through this book?

You could reflect how you are feeling, not in words, but in terms of items and objects chosen and kept in a special box.

The box can serve different purposes. If you feel troubled you can get it out and look at the contents. On another occasion you might show the box to your counsellor.

Your Mood Box

Things that you might put into your box:

- ➢ A favourite CD
- ➢ A beautiful stone
- ➢ Postcards
- ➢ A crystal
- ➢ A stuffed animal
- ➢ Flowers
- ➢ Photographs
- ➢ Material that is pretty or feels nice
- ➢ Jewellery from a loved one
- ➢ Objects from places that hold good memories

Why write anything down?

You might think writing is not an easy thing to do. It does depend on the person, but if you write down things like, 'I can do this', 'I am going to survive this', 'I will accomplish this', there is a real sense of affirmation. In the act of writing it down you are making sense of it to yourself and making it real. This is a strong emotional process.

Your journal

You can also draw things. As you can see, throughout this book there is accompanying artwork that shows how someone is feeling. All the artwork in this book is created by a survivor.

In the journal you can also identify and cancel any negative self-talk. Replace 'I can't', 'I shouldn't', 'I don't dare' with 'I can!', 'I want to!', and 'I will!'.

Being safe

The first creative exercise for the journal is called 'being safe'.

➢ Establish a safe, quiet place where you can work on your journal

➢ Gentle music and incense burners can be used to create a calm atmosphere

➢ You will need to be relaxed there and at ease

➢ You will need to think about your privacy

➢ Who do you want to share the journal with?

What will your journal be like?

_____

_____

_____

_____

_____

_____

_____

_____

_____

_____

_____

_____

_____

_____

_____

_____

_____

_____

_____

_____

CHAPTER 2

SURVIVORS' STORIES

Amber's story

'I was five years old when my Uncle John came to stay with my family. My mum was happy to put her own brother up for a few nights when his marriage broke down. Uncle John was such a help round the house and always prepared to babysit for his little nieces and nephew.

'One night at bath time, Uncle John started to touch me in a way that I did not understand. He told me that it was a secret game, and that I shouldn't tell anyone else about it. I didn't know what was happening.

'I felt confused and didn't really like what Uncle John was doing. After a while Uncle John moved away and I didn't see him for a few years'.

Survivors' stories

Amber was abused as a young girl. When Amber spoke to a counsellor many years later she said, 'I loved my Uncle'. She meant this when she said it, but this does not mean the experience was any less unpleasant or wrong.

'When I was 10, my mum told me that Uncle John had moved back into town and had got his own house with his new girlfriend. My mum was really pleased, especially since Uncle John was keen to have me and the other kids stay over at weekends. I felt absolutely sick at the thought of him coming back. But I did not tell my Mum anything. I did not speak to my Mum because my Uncle had told me that no one would believe me. The abuse started again.

'As I got older, I realised that my Uncle was abusing me, but I felt ashamed that I had not told anyone, and guilty for allowing it to continue. I also felt ashamed that I was unable to say no to the sexual abuse. When I was twelve I started my periods and Uncle John told me that, now I was a woman, we could have proper sex together. I began to cut my arms and body hoping he would not like to see that and leave me alone. Yet he forced me to go to his bed every time I stayed at his house.

'Then I started to have panic attacks. My muscles would tighten and I would sweat and shake. The attacks happened when I least expected them. They affected my concentration at school.

'Uncle John told me that if I didn't let him touch me, then he would have to start on my little sister. I thought that if I allowed the abuse to continue it would protect my sister and at least she could be spared what I had been through. As I got older I started to feel really angry at what my Uncle was doing but didn't know what to do or who to tell'.

Many years later Amber was able to take the first steps on the road to healing.

One of the first things she did in her journal was to acknowledge at what stage she felt she was at in life.

Here are some of her notes. It might be helpful to you to decide what is relevant for you from Amber's journal.

- ➢ Where am I?
- ➢ I remember that I was abused
- ➢ I think I may have been abused
- ➢ I know something happened which changed me
- ➢ I remember what happened and I realise that it affected me
- ➢ I want to deal with what happened
- ➢ I want to deal with my feelings. I will try writing in the journal
- ➢ I have been dealing with my feelings for a long time
- ➢ I want to affirm how far I have come along the road to healing
- ➢ I joined a group and they suggested I keep a journal

Survivors' stories

'When I was fifteen I met a boy called Oliver, at school. Oliver was really thoughtful and gentle and I felt safe when I was with him. I so wanted to be Oliver's girlfriend, but I felt very confused about what was happening with my Uncle.

'I wanted to be loving and intimate with Oliver, but my uncle was still abusing me at this time.

'One day Oliver asked me out and we became a couple. I eventually told Oliver about what had been happening to me. It took a lot of courage to tell him. I was afraid he would reject me. He didn't and in fact was supportive. I could not have asked for more. He was very good at listening. He would be very gentle with me. I told my Uncle that if he did not stop then Oliver would tell the Police. He stopped abusing me at this time'.

In this picture we see Amber isolated from her group of friends. Amber is in emotional torment and unable to communicate her feelings to others. Survivors often expect others around them to notice that they are unhappy or struggling. They assume that everyone else will be as sensitive and alert to suffering as they are themselves.

How do you feel about Amber's story?

SENSITIVE

To be sensitive is to be acutely affected by external stimuli. (The signals people give out that show how they are feeling) Survivors will be generally over-sensitive because of their experiences. Emotions will be heightened. They will find it hard because not everyone will be as sensitive as them.

Many survivors will feel that in social situations they are aware of when people are getting angry or about to have a fight. This is because they can read the atmosphere. This has often been learned from bitter experience.

You can be over-sensitive and obviously this is not a good thing. So what you need to do is to find a balance between being sensitive to other's needs and sensitive to your own needs. You will also be able to be sensitive to other people and see their needs. A survivor can often recognise another survivor without any words being exchanged.

Sensitivity

Actually, unless you say how you are feeling, then no one else can guess what your emotions are. If we are sensitive to others we may be able to recognise when someone is upset. However, it isn't socially acceptable to come out with all your problems. Our communication skills are often sadly lacking. If this is how things are generally, then it is even more difficult when dealing with the subject of abuse.

Many survivors say they can't believe that someone - a neighbour, a teacher, a doctor - didn't notice their misery at the time they endured the abuse. There is more awareness these days of the impact of abuse on a child's behaviour, but children still suffer in silence waiting and hoping for someone to notice their plight.

It is important to listen to children and look for the signs that something may be wrong.

The first step towards becoming aware is noticing when someone is not enjoying themselves, or participating. It cannot be underestimated how even a small positive step towards someone can make all the difference. Every single person can benefit from a smile, and one gesture of recognition. A survivor needs people to be sensitive and positive. This is necessary if they are going to trust someone enough to talk to them.

RAOUL'S STORY

All Raoul's teachers at primary school thought he was badly behaved and disruptive. He found it hard to make friends. The teachers were concerned because he seemed to have strange ideas about his relations with the girls in the class. His teacher suspected that he had been abused because Raoul knew about sexuality in a way that was not appropriate for his age group.

The teacher felt this came out in the language that he used and the way he expressed himself in class. Things came to a head when they were asked to write stories about their families in the lessons.

Raoul seemed very reluctant to undertake the task and did anything to get out of it. He distracted others and kept staring out of the window and twisting his pencil in despair. The teacher asked him why he couldn't write about his family and Raoul just looked at her, and the tears fell down his face.

'I remember the day the teacher forced me to write something about my family, which I found disturbing.'

The teacher noticed that there were bruises on Raoul's arms, which made her suspicious. Later on it was discovered that for some years Raoul had been abused by his own mother.

Raoul could not remember a time when he had not been physically and mentally abused in his family. His mother had many problems and had taken her frustrations out on Raoul. This included sexually abusing him as a small boy.

'I am not the only boy who has been abused by their mother. I tried to win her approval but nothing ever seemed to work.

23

'As I got older I felt trapped in this relationship. It wasn't until I was a bit older that I realised other people and other children at the school had very different home lives. I could see that my home life was threatening, aggressive and inappropriate.

'I kept silent for years, fearing that I would face greater humiliation if I told anyone how I was feeling.

'I was about twelve years old when I found a teacher I could trust and confide in. Then I told that teacher some of the experiences that had happened to me. The teacher was very supportive but I was still living in fear from my mother.

'In time, I was removed to a foster home and it was there I faced all the difficulties that had happened to me. Despite everything that I had endured, to be taken away from my family was very hard to bear.

'As I got older I struggled with conflicting feelings of love and hatred for my mother. I found it hard to make progress towards getting a good job. Then I got in with the wrong crowd and was sometimes led astray. I began living dangerously. I started experimenting with drugs. I put myself and others at risk.'

How do you feel about Raoul's story?

NILES' STORY

Niles was brought up in a strict religious family. When a new priest came to the neighbourhood he became a family friend. Niles' parents were delighted at the attention that Father Bernard showed Niles. Niles felt really moved when Father Bernard showed so much interest in him. Niles was seven years old when he first met Father Bernard. The trust grew and Father Bernard took Niles camping in the countryside. They shared a tent.

At night Niles said he was going to go to sleep. As he undressed Father Bernard stared at him and made no attempt to look away. Niles does not remember any of the details. What he does know is that Father Bernard touched him.

As time went on Father Bernard took the abuse further, on to more intimate acts. Magazines were introduced and Niles was shown images that initiated abuse. During all this time Niles never told anyone what had happened. Niles simply forgot how to feel happy or appreciate life.

When Niles was 17 he had a sexual experience with another boy and then became confused. He wondered if what had happened to him with Father Bernard had made him gay.

This was just one of Niles' worries. He had faced other difficulties and being a survivor was not the end of his life. Niles said, 'The decision I made to heal from my childhood experiences was a positive choice.'

'Healing did not happen overnight. You cannot heal alone, you need to tell someone.

'In the beginning I found it hard to do simple tasks and just get on with my life. For me, each day was dramatic and I felt I was in a crisis.

'I used to walk outside feeling I was getting away from my troubles. I felt there was no point in killing myself. After all, I had survived what Father Bernard had done to me. I was told that how I was feeling was normal. I met other survivors.'

'I was able not to turn to alcohol. There were times when I was reckless with sex because I felt the need for affection. If you were putting yourself at risk like I was then you need to talk to someone. I managed to develop a belief in myself, because I had a good counsellor.

'I felt worried that I had enjoyed what Father Bernard had done to me and this made it impossible to feel attracted to girls. Later

on I decided I was gay and that I could feel positive about that. The counsellor helped me to see that abuse does not determine a person's sexuality. I made a list of things I could do if I felt I was going to get in a panic. I often wrote in my journal, I am safe no one can hurt me now. I do not want to give up. I found that my own will to live gave me hope to go on.

'I can recall some specific times when I was abused by Father Bernard. When I remember, I tell myself it is only a memory. It is not abuse. I used to remember the objects in the room when I was abused, not the abuse itself. Sometimes I do not have images but responses. I was with my partner and they touched me in a particular way and then all the memories came back. It was as if my body had remembered.'

Here we see Niles starting to accept the fact that he is gay

'Sometimes I wonder if the memories are real. When I was watching TV one night I saw a news programme and it said a priest was being arrested for crimes against boys. Then I saw it was Father Bernard. Then it all became very real again. Sometimes I find it hard to believe it all happened to me. I know now that I am not alone when I think that.

'When I was a child, Father Bernard never talked about what he did to me. Now I am able to talk to others about what happened. I broke the silence after 30 years. I had to understand that it was not my fault. I felt I should have been able to stop what was happening. I fell ashamed but I wanted to be close to Father Bernard. He showed me affection. Then there were times when I had an orgasm. I realise now that having an orgasm is the body's normal reaction to stimulation. I can now feel less shame about it.'

Niles' journal

How I feel now:

- ➤ I believe I can be whole again with my partner
- ➤ I found behaviour I wanted to change
- ➤ I found it difficult to form positive sexual experiences
- ➤ I found support
- ➤ I expressed my fears
- ➤ I did not give up
- ➤ I have found a resolution and moved on
- ➤ I feel more stable now
- ➤ I feel I have let go of my crisis
- ➤ I have resolved my relationships
- ➤ There is no final end to my healing
- ➤ I am on a lifetime of growth

How do you feel about Niles' story?

_____

_____

_____

_____

_____

_____

_____

_____

_____

_____

_____

_____

LOOKING AFTER YOURSELF

As you go through this book you will find reminders from Amber, Raoul and Niles. They have had very different and difficult experiences, but they are prepared to share with us what has happened to them and what their lives have been like so that this book has become a journal of their continuing recovery.

As we follow their stories, Amber, Raoul and Niles remind us that we all have to work at making our lives become what we want them to be, and that every choice we make, no matter how small, takes us closer to taking control of our lives and emotions.

How easy is it for you to care for yourself?

When we reached this part of the book, we realised how difficult it was to keep working with such traumatic and upsetting stories. So we are taking a break from the individual stories. When you're feeling down, it's easy to forget the simple everyday things that help you to feel better. It can even be difficult to remember to eat and drink enough, or to bother to take time to prepare nice food.

'I recognise now my feelings as a child. I remember how I felt and I tell that hurt child inside of me that I can hold him and care for him. I take care of the child within and this in turn is a way of nurturing myself.' Niles.

We wanted a way of reminding ourselves and anyone reading this book, that we all need to care and nurture our inner child and ourselves.

Our teddy represents time out for a treat, for a little bit of comfort, for self-preservation and self-love

It is because you are making so many changes in your life that you need to be aware of how important looking after yourself is. You are now letting go of the old ways of coping; you will need to replace those with new, kinder, healthier ideas, beliefs and habits.

Cherish the moments when Teddy appears, because Teddy will be talking about all the things we can do to build ourselves up. Teddy will help us to see the enormous value there is in looking after and caring for ourselves. Teddy represents the healing of the child within us all that has been neglected.

MOTIVATION

You have to be motivated to self-heal. You have to be motivated to make significant progress. To be motivated is to push against any part of you that tries to stop you from doing what you need to do to go forward.

What will motivate you?

Motivation can come from suffering. It is important to recognise that you can turn suffering around and use it to push you forward.

'I will use my life experience to push the boundaries of what I am able to accomplish.' Niles

'YOU EAT LIFE OR LIFE EATS YOU.'
ANON

Survivors

I struggle,
I fight.
I feel I'm right.
I shout,
I cry,
I wish I would die.
I heal,
I grow,
I need you to know,
I love,
I smile,
I survive for a while.

(Keiron Knights, 2004)

You might not think it matters if you don't do anything for yourself, but Teddy represents a vitally important message. If you don't care for yourself, then how can you show caring for anyone else? If you aren't able to give yourself love then how will you know how to share it with anyone else?

You have choices and responsibilities.

These include a responsibility to yourself. Children have to be taught how to recognise when they are hungry, when they need to wash, when to have a rest. Now that you are an adult you may not have learnt those things. You may have learnt those values and neglect them. You have to relearn the value in caring for yourself.

No one else can do that for you.

That may sound harsh, but it is the truth. No one else can know your inner needs. You have to learn to treat your inner child as if they were real.

You're never too big to have a Teddy to love

We think everyone should have a cuddly teddy to remind you to love yourself, to care for yourself and to nurture yourself. To say, 'What are you doing now to make yourself feel better?'

Teddy can be that good friend who will insist that you treat yourself with respect and dignity. Hopefully, if you take some of this advice, you will start to feel much better.

You do not need an actual teddy. You do not need to buy anything to access this sense of comfort. It is about recognising that you need comforting, and then giving yourself permission to comfort yourself. Maybe you have a safe place in your own home, where you need to go to feel safe. It is about recognising what the inner child's need is.

When you are upset what do you need?

Do you need to sit quietly with a drink?

Do you need to tell a friend?

Do you need to go for a walk?

Do you snuggle down in a blanket?

This is not ridiculous at all. Taking care of yourself is a necessary part of healing.

Teddy pops up quite a lot through the book, to tell you that you need to be constantly asking yourself: 'How have I cared for myself today?'

Raoul's Journal

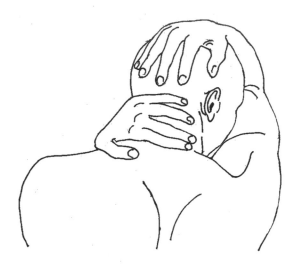

Drawing made by Raoul when he was feeling very low

Here is an example of a poem that Raoul included in his journal.

'Who's that? Why stare?

What you doing there?

You got no business out on the street

Strutting round for any innocent to meet.

But I know you're still banged up inside

You took a lot, but not my pride.

Always thought I'd beat you up,

But I was scared – ain't got no guts.

But you won't win, I didn't do no sin.

No blame on me, No shame on me.

I've made my peace, and now I'm free.'

Now you have an example of the kind of writing that you could do in your journal. The above example is taken from Raoul's journal. You will learn more about Raoul later on, when you hear more of his story.

'I remember how I felt when I did this page in my journal. I just wanted to take it out on everyone - and myself most of all. I was so angry at everyone and everything. All those bad feelings were wrecking my life. It's a real reminder of how much I've changed. I don't know what would have happened to me if I'd just held on to those feelings.'

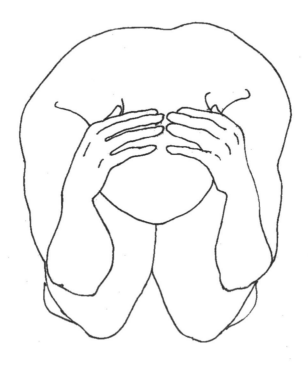

Survivors' stories

'I have done other drawings which show a far more positive attitude. I think this is a good exercise to do. It's about letting out your feelings and being able to move on. Its very good if you can't be bothered to write sentences.' Raoul

Time for your Journal

Really, the only way to keep an effective journal is to take time out to write it, or choose an item for your mood box. 10 to 15 minutes a day is a good reflective time to spend evaluating how you are feeling. Like we've already said, some people find writing down much easier than others. If you prefer, you could just put down bullet points – a few words showing how you feel.

 *How do you feel about setting out on your own healing journey?*

_____

_____

_____

_____

_____

_____

_____

_____

_____

_____

_____

_____

NEGATIVE SELF-TALK

The real meaning of words

Words have the power to communicate what we are thinking and feeling. Through words we can describe our world and our lives. We use words in our own thoughts to tell ourselves what is happening and how we feel. This is why words are so powerful.

If we constantly use negative words, then this affects how we are thinking and feeling. This is called negative self-talk. Survivors often have a whole dictionary of negative words to describe themselves and their lives, which they use many times each day. The impact of this on someone's sense of self-worth is huge.

Would you constantly criticise a friend or colleague in the same way that you use negative self-talk to criticise yourself? We sincerely hope you would be much kinder and more thoughtful, and would find words that supported and encouraged them. You might think about why they aren't happy or aren't coping as well as they could. You might more easily forgive them for being short-tempered or grumpy. We are only asking you to give yourself the same respect and thought that you would give to someone else.

Here are some examples from Amber, Raoul and Niles of the ways they have talked about themselves. As you're reading their journals you can ask yourself whether what they've actually said is accurate. You might say that you have to trust what people have to say about themselves. Yet, we know that if somebody doesn't point out to you that you might be using negative self-talk you will be completely unaware of it. In all three cases, they have now realised how negative they had been before they started healing.

AMBER'S JOURNAL

1. My feelings
   I can't control my feelings.

2. Self-belief
   I don't believe I can do anything.

3. Body image
   I hate my body.

4. Intimacy
   Why would anyone want me?

5. Relationships
   No-one can love me now.

6. Sexuality
   Sex is dirty.

7. My family
   My family didn't care about me because they wanted a boy.

8. Being a parent
   I don't think I could be a parent because I wouldn't be able to cope.

9. My achievements
   Everything always goes wrong for me.

10. My future
    My future can't be very exciting because of the person I am.

RAOUL'S JOURNAL

1. My feelings
    It's weak to think about having feelings.

2. Self-belief
    No good, never been any good, never will be any good.

3. My body image
    Why should I care what the drugs might do to my body?

4. Intimacy
    I'm oversexed. Sex doesn't mean anything.

5. Relationships
    I'm not very good at relationships.

6. Sexuality
    Sex always involves aggression.
    Sex always hurts.

7. My family
    My family are worthless.

8. Being a parent
    I don't know if I can be a good parent.

9. My achievements
    The kind of person I am doesn't have achievements.

10. My future
    Keeping out of prison, if I can.

NILES' JOURNAL

1. My feelings
   If I feel too happy, something will go wrong.

2. Self-belief
   If people knew what I was like they wouldn't want to know me.

3. My body image
   My body is ugly.

4. Intimacy
   I can never know what love is.

5. Relationships
   I'll never have a long-term relationship.

6.   Sexuality
   I think I'm ashamed of being gay.

7. My family
   I'm not the son my father wanted.

8. Being a parent
   I could never be a good parent.

9. My achievements
   The only thing I've achieved is having a job.

10. My future
    I don't really think about my future.

Here you might like to outline the negative self-talk you may have used about yourself

1. My feelings

2. Self-belief

3. My body image

4. Intimacy

5. Relationships

6. Sexuality

_____

_____

7. Being a parent

_____

_____

8. My family

_____

_____

9. My achievements

_____

_____

10. My future

_____

_____

_____

_____

POSITIVE SELF TALK

Throughout the book there are words and descriptions. If you look at these words they might inspire you. We are not suggesting that you need to take them all on board – it might not be right for you, or it might not be the right time for it – but they can suggest to you all sorts of possibilities for focusing your thoughts and feelings. See if you can take some of these words on board in your own life, through writing them down in your journal.

EFFECTIVE

You can be effective in your chosen path. You have the confidence and ability to focus on your goal to be healed.

'I realise now that for years I would not accept any positive encouragement for myself. This did not allow me to be as effective as I can be now that I have been through the process of healing.' Amber

---

'What if I really tried to be effective?'

Survivors' stories

Keep a record in your journal of the words you choose to encourage yourself - what it means to you, how they might apply to you and, how you would like them to apply to you.

Every person is different, and you can choose whether or not the suggestions fit in with your own situation.

You can give yourself permission to be any of the words that you choose. No one can stop you.

In time you may come back to the book again and find different words and different concepts that sustain your sense of self-worth.

 *What positive words would you like to use to describe yourself?*

_____

_____

_____

_____

_____

_____

_____

_____

BELIEF

This is the single most powerful concept in this book. If you believe that you can succeed then you will. If you believe that you can make progress then you will. In the treatment of AIDS for example, doctors have found patients' positive belief in themselves to influence the regression of the disease.

Patients are encouraged to talk to the healthy T-cells in their body. When a person has done this believing themselves able to influence their physical body the T-cell count can be maintained. Those patients who have little or no self-belief will see their T-cell count to go down. This is done by patients looking at themselves in a mirror and talking to themselves positively and encouraging the good T-cell count to multiply. Doctors have verified that a positive attitude can directly influence the physical condition of a patient.

'It took me years to believe in myself.' Niles

PROGRESSIVE

You need to believe in the idea of progress. This is important because we can all make progress and see that we are moving in a line and not in a circle.

'I never thought I would have made such progress in my relationships.' Raoul

At this point it might be a good idea to take the time to outline the positive messages that you want to give yourself – at this stage you are reviewing and self-evaluating your journey

My feelings

_____

_____

Self-belief

_____

_____

My body image

_____

_____

Intimacy

_____

_____

_____

Relationships

_____

_____

Sexuality

_____

_____

Being a parent

_____

_____

My family

_____

_____

My achievements

_____

_____

My future

_____

_____

KEEP GROUNDED

While you are working on healing, it will be important to keep yourself grounded in the present. You may find that your traumatic memories intrude into your thoughts even more, simply because you are focusing on the past. It is particularly useful to ground yourself if you find you have been having intrusive thoughts or traumatic memories and is a good way of connecting back to the here and now.

Here the wizard is telling you to make a conscious decision to want to get grounded and feel as if you are in the present more often than you may be at this time.

You will find that grounding yourself like this can even help if you start to feel panicky.

What does 'keeping grounded' mean?

Well, grounded means when you are feeling solidly and securely in today – not sad or angry about the past, nor worrying about tomorrow. You need to keep grounded so that your mind and body are reacting to what is actually happening now in the present. That means your thoughts, physical sensations, emotional and behavioural responses are all appropriate to the current situation.

GROUNDED

This means having a real connection to our emotions, thoughts and sensations so that our feelings reflect our understanding of what is actually happening, and we can react appropriately.

Some survivors say they are not always grounded. They feel as if they are not always in the present. This can happen at anytime or when they engage in consensual sexual activity. In order to be grounded you need to feel as if you are in the present all the time. It will help you to get into a healing programme so that this can happen.

TRY THIS EXERCISE NOW

Focus carefully on your surroundings, noticing all the different objects around you and all the different sounds you can hear. **Then choose one object to focus on. Think really hard about the object – look at its shape and colour.**

- ➢ What is it made of?
- ➢ How has it been made?
- ➢ What is it used for?

Now turn this focus inside your body for a few seconds.

- ➢ Can you feel any tension in your body?
- ➢ What feelings or words come into your mind when you focus on that tension?
- ➢ What is your inner child telling you?

Now turn your focus outside again, and look around you. Connect back up to where you are.

Finally, remind yourself of the present day and date. You are safe now.

What are the feelings that you noticed?

- ➢ Are they relevant to what is happening today?
- ➢ Do they belong in the past?
- ➢ Are they appropriate feelings for what is happening?

You have now grounded yourself – your physical sensations and your emotions – in what is happening right now, in the present day. You may find that the feelings you recognised in yourself do not match what is happening? If not, can you connect them to another time in the past?

MOOD SWINGS

The first thing our Wizards are going to do is to remind you about checking your feelings. One of the big problems for survivors is mood swings – feeling out of control and overreacting to everyday situations. Maybe you recognise this in yourself? The situation may be any everyday event, and is often quite trivial. For example, the parking space that someone just nips into before you. Or it might be something simple like a spilt drink, or broken cup.

A survivor often experiences their biggest problems in relationships, by over-reacting to their partner. This is often because they are reacting by losing their temper over trivial incidents.

Aristotle, a Greek philosopher said that anger should be treated with respect. It has to be for the right reason, aimed at the right target, to the right proportion and for the right purpose. Used correctly, anger is a wonderful emotion that rights wrongs, motivates all kinds of personal and social improvements, protects children, wins wars – it even gets whales and foxes saved! It is OK to be angry but not to take it out on the wrong target.

DECISIVE

You have made a decision to be healed and this will be your focus for some time now, until you feel better about yourself.

'There were times when I couldn't even decide what flavour yoghurt to buy for the kids. I had to reassure myself that I was going through a difficult time and that I was bound to feel unsure of making any decisions. I found it helped if I could ground myself and then rate the decision I was trying to make on a scale of one to ten – one being unimportant and ten being vital. 'Number one' decisions were much easier then – we only ever had strawberry yoghurt for ages, but we survived. 'Number ten' decisions were still difficult, but they always would have been.' Amber

If you are constantly feeling annoyed at the slightest thing, or taking your moods out on someone close to you, then you and your loved ones are at the mercy of unhappy emotions coming from past experiences. This is what is meant by unresolved emotions, often feelings of shame or guilt or even anger, towards oneself.

Imagine carrying a huge bowl, full to the brim of water, around with you everywhere. Just a few drops more added to the bowl will make the water overflow, and even a little stumble will spill water everywhere. Its exhausting carrying the heavy bowl everywhere, you can't control it and its impossible not to spill water everywhere.

Now imagine that the bowl you are carrying is full of all the unresolved emotions you have from the past. The slightest upset or difficulty causes all the emotions to spill out. What you end up with is the emotional response to what is actually happening today, but also all the emotional baggage that falls out of the bowl with it as well.

You will know yourself when you're going over the top in whatever situation. It takes time and practice to regain control of your emotions, but you can do it! What you need to do is to watch what is happening when you go over the top in your reactions.

Mood swings checklist

Go through this checklist as soon as you find yourself getting into a situation where you might over-react:

➢ Stop – ground yourself

➢ How do you feel?

➢ Think things through

➢ Choose how to react

➢ Check out how you did

1. STOP.

Slow everything down as much as you can. Taking time to think things through gives you control over how you react and what you say and do.

Stop the activity. This might mean that you have to ask someone else to stop what they are doing as well.

2. HOW DO YOU FEEL?

Give yourself time to work out what emotion you are feeling. Ground yourself. Ask yourself these questions:

Is this the appropriate feeling for what is actually happening?

Is how I am feeling in proportion to what has happened?

3. THINK THINGS THROUGH.

What is the most important thing in what is happening to me at this time?

What do you want to happen next?

4. CHOOSE HOW TO REACT

Now you have thought about what you want to happen, you can choose what you say or do that will help work towards this.

5. CHECK OUT HOW YOU DID

You will have to work at changing behaviour and thinking patterns that have usually ended up in situations where you over-react. If you feel you haven't managed to react how you really wanted to, then use this as a way of learning so that next time you will have more control.

Ask yourself:

How have I coped?

How could I cope differently?

Sexual violence and abuse create strong emotions in everyone, but these can often get confused – sadness, rage, fear, revenge, suspicion, hatred, self-loathing – all jumbled together so that it's impossible to work out what reaction is relevant to what is happening in the present. Once you have regained control of your emotions, then you can start to choose what you do and start to feel the power of making your own choices in your everyday life.

BASIC HUMAN RIGHTS

Before we go any further it might be helpful to:

Remember! Basic Human Rights.

One of the first things you can do to start challenging negative feelings is to remind yourself that everyone has basic rights. In sexual, physical or emotional abuse those rights are totally ignored.

We may all feel isolated at some point. We know we can't dare tell how we really feel because if we did we would be discovered to be vulnerable, and that, society says, is considered a weakness.

This is a lot of what this book is about – to challenge this stereotype.

Even this is not enough. We would like to go even further, to attempt to show how to heal the pain. We asked ourselves, 'How can we find the way to the door of inner happiness that can lead us into the light of healing?' We decided that we had to start by affirming everyone's basic human rights.

Sometimes, when you have experienced trauma, it can be difficult for you to believe that you actually have the same basic rights as everyone else. You may fully understand the concept of human rights, but believe that it relates to everyone else and that you yourself are somehow different – different because of the trauma you have experienced and because of how you have responded to it.

You may blame yourself and feel guilty. You may even recognise that because of your experiences you have behaved and reacted in ways that aren't positive.

Well, we all, regardless of what has happened or will happen, have basic human rights. This applies equally to adults and to children. In our society we need to constantly affirm those rights for each other:

> ➢ The right to grow up and develop free from fear and guilt
> ➢ The right to be protected from harm, abuse and violence
> ➢ The right to learn what is right and what is wrong
> ➢ A right to be treated as equal to everyone else, with respect and dignity
> ➢ The right to be treated in a way that is sensitive of race, class, religion, sexual orientation or disability
> ➢ The right to express our own opinions and values
> ➢ The right to choose YES or NO without feeling guilty
> ➢ The right to make mistakes

**Survivors have a right to be listened to and believed.
We can't say this often enough**

DO BOYS REACT DIFFERENTLY?

Now we return to Raoul's story.

'I wanted to join in the fun with the lads. I felt unable to because I was unhappy. I had low self-esteem. I had been sexually abused by my mother.

'I had the physical scars on my body from where my mum hit me. I did not want to take my shirt off in front of the other boys.' Raoul

Many lads who are abused are not going to find it easy to tell anyone about it.

Some people who work in specialist voluntary sector agencies believe that just as many boys are abused each year as are girls.

Boys can respond differently to trauma than girls. This is serious because boys are generally not as communicative as girls and tend to bottle up their emotions.

Girls more often internalise their feelings as depression whilst boys more often express their emotional response as anger.

It is a fact that the highest numbers of all suicides recorded are for young men.

This shows that boys have some difficulty dealing with emotions. Boys generally tend to respond in a more outwardly dramatic fashion to trauma than girls. However, you would be wrong to make the assumption that all males react in the same way. Men with many different temperaments have been victims of sexual abuse.

Raoul is typical of someone who will find an outlet for his feelings. In boys the expression of disgust with what has happened to them might be violent. Raoul might in fact hurt others or be aggressive. Girls might also have this violent response, but it is more likely that boys might become aggressive or violent with others.

The younger the child at the time of the abuse, the more profound the damage can be. Raoul may have behaviour that will never be understood unless in the context of his traumatic experiences. If he never unlocks his past, the effects will remain with him. In fact, it will stay with him night and day.

VALUED

We all need to feel valued. When we value ourselves, then others also value us. Value can come from attachment to others. If we can feel of some value to others then this can keep perspective on ourselves. Ask yourself what do you value most? Make a list.

'I didn't feel I could value myself. Yet now I cherish the fact that I can value myself and others, especially my partner.' Raoul

'I would tell any man who has experienced sexual abuse to find himself a good support network. It can be embarrassing to admit that you have been abused, because it makes you feel weak. As though you aren't manly. I think that's why I used to take it out on everyone else. That's why support groups are so important.' Raoul

CHAPTER 3

DEFINITIONS OF RAPE AND SEXUAL ABUSE

YOU DON'T HAVE TO READ THIS SECTION NOW – ITS OKAY TO COME BACK TO IT LATER

When we were writing this chapter, we realised how difficult it was for us to spend so much time concentrating on such challenging subjects. However, we felt that it was important that these definitions were included. You might feel that you don't need to be told any definitions – you've lived with the problems – or you may welcome the opportunity to read our definitions of what rape and abuse involve so that you can think more clearly about your own experiences. As we were writing, though, we made sure we had regular coffee breaks and sometimes we decided to leave a section for later. It's okay for you to do this too as a positive choice to nurture yourself.

WHAT IS SEXUAL ABUSE?

Sexual abuse is when someone is touched or looked at or spoken to in a sexual way that makes them feel uncomfortable. In fact, any sexual behaviour that is not mutual and where free choice is not possible is sexually abusive. The kinds of behaviour that are sexually abusive include:

> ➢ Looking or staring at someone, so that they feel uncomfortable

> ➢ Inappropriate sexual talk

> ➢ Touching or stroking, including touching someone's genitals

> ➢ Holding or kissing

> ➢ Masturbation – making a child masturbate themselves or someone else, including another child

> ➢ Oral sex

> ➢ Statutory rape

> ➢ Taking indecent or pornographic photographs or films

> ➢ Forcing or coercing a child/adult to have sex with another child/adult against their will

> ➢ Forcing or coercing a child/adult to engage in sexual activity with objects or animals against their will

> ➢ Rape of a child or adult

> ➢ Ritualised abuse of a child/adult

With children, a relationship is deemed to be abusive if one person is five or more years older than someone under the age of sixteen. Choice is the most important aspect in deciding if sexual abuse has taken place. Some young people under sixteen develop relationships with older boyfriends or girlfriends where sexual intercourse takes place. Technically this is against the law. In practice, as long as it is a mutual relationship, and no complaint is made, then there are times when the police will take no action.

WHAT IS STATUTORY RAPE?

If a child is under the age of thirteen, and sexual intercourse has taken place then it is regarded in law as statutory rape.

This can result in a prison sentence unless it can be proven that the older person had good reason to believe that they were over the age of thirteen.

However, the important thing to recognise is the person's feelings in any given situation. If someone feels that an experience has been abusive for them, then that is their experience and the impact on them will be traumatic.

WHAT IS RAPE?

Can you stop talking about it now. . .?

Take a break if you need to

In 2004 The Sexual Offences Act became law and changed the legal definition of rape. Rape is now used to describe the penetration of a person's body, either vaginally, orally or anally, by a penis.

Most rapes in fact happen in the home. Twenty five percent of rapes involve children. The vast majority of these rapes go unreported.

Definitions of rape and sexual abuse

The definition of rape has changed over time. It wasn't until 1992 that it became a crime for a married man to rape his wife. Before this many women were raped by their husbands. It was seen as a husband's right to claim sex from his wife. Today a married woman has the right not to be taken advantage of in her marriage.

Gay men have the right to report rape within a partnership. However because of the nature of the act, society doesn't easily accept it, and gay men may feel they will not necessarily be believed.

It does not matter how many partners a person has had or what their sexual history is. No one wants or deserves to be raped. This includes where they went, or what they were wearing or who they were with. It also includes if they knew the person or if they had had consensual sex with that person before.

Male Rape

There are strong social barriers in the reporting of a male rape and most cases are not reported. This includes when the victims are young boys. Most men will suffer the indignity and pain in silence. Society expects men to be strong and self-sufficient. Generally, there is resistance in society to believing male rape happens. However, it is important for everyone to understand that men do get raped, by other men, and also sometimes by women.

Unfortunately, there are some mistaken beliefs in society about male rape. It is often generally believed that only gay men get raped and that men who rape other men must be gay themselves. Neither of these beliefs is true, but these myths can get in the way of a man seeking help and also influence how a man feels about himself following an assault.

In the vast majority of cases, the men who rape other men are heterosexual and both homosexual and heterosexual men get raped. This emphasizes the fact that rape is not driven by a sexual urge, but rather by a drive to control and hold power over someone else. It is an aggressive act of dominance and has absolutely nothing to do with passion or lust.

A man who has experienced rape will have many of the same feelings and responses of a woman who has been raped. However, there are some additional pressures that a man might experience. There are far fewer support resources for male survivors, so men have can have great difficulty in finding support immediately following an assault. A man may feel that the police will not take him seriously. Perhaps the most difficult feeling for a man who has been raped is that his masculinity has been cast into doubt. A fear response can provoke an erection in a man, and this may cause some men to question their own sexuality.

Homophobic abuse

In some circumstances gay men are abused by other men to humiliate and degrade them. Incidents include anal or oral rape. Often the attacks involve more than one person. The rapists are not gay, and justify their actions through homophobic rage. In attacks like this, the physical and verbal abuse can be much higher than in other rape incidents.

Male rape in prison

In an informal survey of prison officers, the results showed that, in their experience, up to 80% of the men in prison have experienced sexual abuse at some time. In prison there are some reported incidences of rape. However, it is known that many are not reported. It may be that rape is used in prison to humiliate and degrade prisoners. It might be that men who go into prison will be heterosexual, but inside they will adopt predatory and aggressive homosexual practices. It might be that men will have to offer sexual favours because of circumstances, and this makes them vulnerable.

Date Rape

Date rape is a term that has been used to describe when someone is raped by a person they have met on a date or whom they may have known for some time. In this situation people can often feel unable to report the crime. This is because they know the person and feel that they are less likely to be believed.

There is also the social aspect, that if you go out with someone on a date there is some expectation that sex might occur. This acts as a contributing factor in certain rapes not being reported. There are many incidences in the newspapers where the prosecution is unsuccessful.

If you have been out with someone who is in your social circle and you claim they have raped you, there can be huge consequences. You could find that your mutual friends cannot believe that someone they know is capable of rape. You might lose your friends at a time when you need them most. There have been many such examples of this happening.

Date Rape Drugs

Date Rape Drugs are used by an abuser to make someone physically helpless and to make them unable to refuse sex. The term 'date rape drugs' is misleading, however, because the drugs are more commonly used in many situations other than when someone is 'on a date'. These drugs will make someone lose their inhibitions and they will also be unable to remember what has happened. Both women and men are at risk, especially in pubs and clubs where drinks may be left unattended. The effects of the drugs will vary depending on the amount of the drug that has been taken and whether it is mixed with anything else, like alcohol, which can make the effects worse.

There are three main drugs associated with sexual assaults and rape - GHB (gamma hydroxybutyric acid), Rohypnol and Ketamine:

GHB (gama hydroxybutyric acid)

This may be in the form of either a clear, odourless liquid, a pill or white powder. Although it is used to treat sleep disorders, it can actually be made quite easily in someone's home – in this case, it is impossible to know exactly what has been put into the drug. Sometimes GHB can have a salty taste. The drug passes through the body in twelve hours and is therefore very difficult to test for.

The effects of GHB can include:

> ➢ Feeling extremely relaxed and sleepy
> ➢ Feeling dizzy and nauseous
> ➢ Breathing difficulties
> ➢ Blacking out
> ➢ Seizures
> ➢ Loss of memory
> ➢ Sweating and shaking
> ➢ Problems with vision
> ➢ Vomiting
> ➢ Slow heart rate
> ➢ Coma and even death

Definitions of rape and sexual abuse

Rohypnol (flunitrazepam)

Rohypnol comes in pill form which dissolves in liquids. Manufacturers have now produced pills that turn blue when added to liquids, but there are still old pills available.

It can be used to treat sleep disorders and also as an anaesthetic to relieve pain during surgery. Rohypnol leaves no trace in the body after 72 hours.

The effects of rohypnol include:

- ➢ Feeling drunk very quickly not related to the number of alcoholic drinks someone has had
- ➢ Dizziness and confusion
- ➢ Problems with vision
- ➢ Feeling sleepy
- ➢ Loss of memory
- ➢ Not being able to walk and talk properly
- ➢ Feeling sick and stomach problems

Ketamine (ketamine hydrochloride)

Ketamine is an anaesthetic for both humans and animals but is used mainly by veterinary surgeons. It comes in the form of a white powder.

The effects of ketamine include:

- ➢ Hallucinations
- ➢ Problems walking and talking
- ➢ Vomiting
- ➢ Loss of memory
- ➢ Out of body experiences
- ➢ Increased sex drive

> ➢ Convulsions and numbness

> ➢ Breathing difficulties

Generally, the drugs are added to someone's drink and because they do not have any odour or colour they are undetectable to taste or smell.

More recently, there have been instances where formaldehyde has been soaked into cigarettes. When the cigarettes are smoked the effects are similar to those listed for the three drugs above.

Some people would classify alcohol as a drug that can be used to facilitate rape or sexual abuse. The effects of alcohol can be:

> ➢ Lowering of inhibitions

> ➢ Slurred speech

> ➢ Loss of consciousness

> ➢ Being unable to walk

> ➢ Loss of memory

An abuser may give a child alcohol to make them quiet or compliant and to disrupt memories.

What to do if you think you have been drugged and raped?

> ➢ Contact the nearest Sexual Assault Referral Centre (contact numbers listed in page 327). These Centres will provide immediate support and will also ensure that any forensic evidence is gathered and stored properly. This does not mean that you will have to press charges, but allows you the choice of taking further action at a later date if you do want to. The SARC will also be able to run tests for drugs. You can contact the SARC yourself or through the police

> ➢ Although it is the first thing you might want to do, don't bathe or change your clothes before seeking help. This will enable forensic evidence to be preserved

> ➢ Don't urinate (or if you have to, then collect the urine in a clean container) – the drugs leave the body very quickly and will show up in urine for only a short time

> ➢ Contact a local rape crisis support group – the National Rape and Childhood Sexual Abuse Helpline will provide contact details of your nearest centre. The support group will often provide someone who can support you immediately and accompany you to the SARC, GP or police

REMEMBER no-one has the right to assault someone else. You are not to blame. It is normal to feel guilty and ashamed after an assault, but actually you have the right to decide who touches your body and in what circumstances. Nothing can detract from that right. Even if you have taken other drugs or alcohol, you still have that right.

Gang rape

In some circumstances rape occurs where more than one person participates in the rape. This can involve male and female rapists. In a gang situation some people can participate in the rape by holding the victim down. They may not participate in the raping itself, but they are as guilty for inciting rape. In these situations rape is defined as any violation of the body.

Gang rape more often involves a male victim rather than female victim. Often multiple sexual acts are perpetrated, and it is more common for weapons to be used. Male victims are likely to have more serious injuries than female victims who are injured.

WHO ARE THE ABUSERS?

Most of us will imagine that abusers are people who are unpleasant and undesirable. This is far from the truth. You can't see them by walking down the street. It is not obvious.

There are people who 'flash' themselves at others. These people expose themselves to unsuspecting members of the public. They are called flashers. Then there are the abductors. We all think these sort of people are dirty and monsters. In fact such cases, while upsetting, are not typical of people who abuse. It is rare that anyone will be abused by a perfect stranger.

It is far more likely to be someone who is known. That is the first shock. Not only known, but it is often a member of a family. Fathers, mothers, aunts, uncles, brothers and cousins, even friends could be possible candidates. Sometimes even a grandparent can abuse.

In some families, there are generations of the family involved in abuse: grandparents, parents, uncles and aunts all involved in abusing the children of the family.

Some paedophiles actually seek out vulnerable families (maybe where a mother or father are coping with children on their own) and will be extremely patient in cultivating the trust of the whole family simply so that they can get close to a child. This can be very difficult to take on board.

It seems so unlikely that someone would wait years, but that is what some paedophiles are prepared to do. In fact, what they are often doing is waiting for a child to reach the age that they prefer to abuse a child at. They may have several children that they are 'grooming' at the same time.

Research has shown that an abuser will commit on average 250 offences before being caught. Someone who abuses one child will, more likely than not, also abuse others, often many others. Their behaviour is persistent and does not slow down as they get older.

Definitions of rape and sexual abuse

We are now discovering that sexually abusive behaviour often starts in adolescence and, if not treated soon enough or appropriately, will persist into adult life.

Sadly, people in authority like religious leaders or teachers can, and have, abused children. Then there are those people who socially have had the trust and respect of youngsters.

So many youngsters have respected priests or social workers, who have rewarded this respect with abuse. We may feel, on hearing this, that we want to change society. If only we could.

Most people who are raped are attacked in their own homes. They are more likely to know the person who rapes them. Often it will be a husband, partner or boyfriend.

Most rapists are socially inadequate. They often have poor relationships with others and are unable to maintain fulfilling adult relationships.

In the case of stranger rapes, where sadistic violence is used, then often the attack has been planned – the area will have been carefully considered, and the victim may have been chosen and watched for some time.

Although there is a lot of fear generated in the media about stranger rapes, they account for only two percent of all reported rapes.

UNBALANCED GENDER ROLES

When we look at society, we see that problems are linked with the different expectations we have for men and women. It is a sad fact that most rapists are male. Most violent sexual abuse is male. A paedophile is most likely to be male. Why is this? What is it about being male that means someone is more likely to be abusive? We do not really know. What is happening to men in our society that causes this?

When males are growing up they are given lots of messages by society that in order to be true men they must show 'manly' qualities, then they must take the opposite approach to women. The following activities are discouraged for developing males:

> Nurturing is considered a female activity. Caring for anyone is a female activity, whether babies, children, old people or the sick

> Rearing children is a female activity, and that includes teaching. Many males do not take kindly to bringing up children. Many males run away from this aspect of life. Abuse is the opposite to nurturing others

> Talking to people, developing a conversation, or having a discussion are all considered female activities

> Expressing emotions. Many males have difficulties expressing their emotions. They do not speak and so bottle up their feelings

> Reading and writing are sedate activities – men are active. Males are the hunters, out making conquests

> Loving, trusting and being romantic are considered female traits. Males are supposed to like the lust factor. They just go out and have sex

> Doing well at studies in school is a female trait

> Artistic interests, the arts and literature are feminine activities

Definitions of rape and sexual abuse

On the other hand, some activities are specifically associated with being a man:

- ➢ Aggressive behaviour
- ➢ Violent outbursts
- ➢ Frustration
- ➢ Harm of children is male
- ➢ Domestic violence
- ➢ Power games

Some of the consequences of this unbalanced sharing of gender roles and activities seem to be:

- ➢ The male ego is fragile
- ➢ The male has no language available to express himself
- ➢ Males are prone to be homophobic. In the past gay men have been murdered in what often appears to be homophobic attacks
- ➢ Males easily accept lesbian relationships but feel threatened by homosexual ones
- ➢ The highest suicide rate in society is among young males

Somehow, we are failing our children when we nurture in them the same old patterns of behaviour that we have had to conform to ourselves. Somehow, as a whole society, we need to heal the gap between the genders so that everyone can learn to respect and value others for their personal qualities rather than their biological sexes.

There are women who abuse others. In many ways it can be more shocking because women are thought to have a nurturing nature. This can make it harder for someone to disclose that a woman has abused them.

Women can be involved in abuse by remaining silent when they know it is happening. This is clearly wrong. They can be involved in procuring victims for another. This is also morally wrong.

SHOCKING STATISTICS

The generally accepted figures are that one in four girls are sexually abused before the age of eighteen.

Many people do not realise that one in six boys will also suffer from sexual abuse before the age of eighteen as well.

How real is this?

This is probably a conservative estimate. The vast majority of people who are abused never report it to anyone.

A confidential telephone survey commissioned by Dublin Rape Crisis in Ireland revealed that one in three adults reported that they had been sexually abused at some time in their lives. (The SAVI Report)[1]

Statistics cited in the DABS Resource Directory (see page 323) reveal that one million children (approximately) are abused in some way in the UK each year.

50% of those abused as children, who are now adults, never reported the abuse.

In 67% of cases the abuse started before the age of 11 years of age and lasted between 2-18 years.

(These are the reported cases. Therefore the actual figures are probably higher.)

---

[1] The SAVI Report, Sexual Abuse and Violence in Ireland. A National Study of Irish Experiences, Beliefs and Attitudes Concerning Sexual Violence. Hannah McGee, Rebecca Garavan, Mairéad de Barra, Joanne Byrne, Ronán Conroy

EMOTIONAL AND PSYCHOLOGICAL WELLBEING

Research findings quoted in a Briefing Paper prepared for The Survivors Trust[2], are now starting to show what the devastating impact can be. Abuse can affect a person's whole life in every aspect of their existence:

> ➢ Adults who were sexually abused in childhood are more likely to be victims of domestic violence

> ➢ One study found that almost half (48.9%) of childhood sexual abuse victims become victims of a violent partner as an adult. This compared to 17.6% of non-victims of childhood sexual abuse

General health

> ➢ Exposure to traumatic events such as sexual abuse and assault can be related to poor physical health. Post Traumatic Stress Disorder (PTSD), which is a common mental health symptom of childhood sexual abuse and rape, is also related to health problems

> ➢ There is not yet sufficient evidence to conclusively show a direct cause and effect between trauma/PTSD and poor physical health, but a number of studies have noted the association

> ➢ Particular physical health problems that have been reported in studies are cancer, ischaemic heart disease, chronic lung disease, hypertension and other cardiovascular symptoms, abnormalities in thyroid and other hormone functions, increased susceptibility to infections, immunological disorders, gastrointestinal and musculoskeletal disorders

[2] the Inter-relatedness of Sexual Victimisation and Priority Social and Health Policy Issues, A Briefing from The Survivors Trust, Kathryn Livingston, 2004

Mental health

➢ 50 – 60% of psychiatric inpatients and 40 – 60% of outpatients were physically and/or sexually abused as children

➢ 50 – 80% of women who are raped develop post-traumatic stress disorder (compared to 5 – 8% of combat veterans)

➢ Men and boys who are sexually assaulted are more likely to suffer from post-traumatic stress disorder, anxiety disorders and depression than those who have never been abused sexually

Self-belief

➢ Adults who experienced childhood sexual abuse are 12 times more likely to attempt suicide than those who did not

➢ Sexually abused young men are amongst the highest risk groups for youth suicide

Crime and anti-social behaviour

➢ A UK study published in The Lancet showed that 88% of men who were abused in childhood did not become abusers in adulthood

➢ Of the minority that were convicted of a sexual offence in adulthood, there were specific factors additional to the fact that they were themselves abused, which increased the risk of becoming an abuser

➢ Victims of child sexual abuse are 27.7 times more likely to be arrested for prostitution as adults than non-victims

Negative coping strategies

> ➢ A survey of 47 drug addiction agencies in Scotland estimated that 50% of their clients had been abused in childhood

> ➢ 67 – 90% of women with alcohol and drug addiction problems are survivors of childhood sexual abuse

> ➢ Adult male victims of childhood sexual abuse are significantly more likely than their non-abused counterparts to meet the criteria for substance use disorder (55.5% versus 26.7% respectively) or for drug abuse/dependence (44.9% versus 7.8% respectively)

> ➢ One study proposes that individuals will often choose and use drugs which manage specific effects and consequences of abuse (such as intrusive recollections, flashbacks, nightmares, avoidance, numbing or hyper-vigilance)

Preventing abuse

Psychologists and the police might say that people who abuse others are behaving in an evil way. But often the people who are being abusive are partners and family members. In other aspects of their lives, they may be able to be responsible and caring. There is only a tiny minority of abusers and rapists who might fit into the category of 'evil'.

We now know that many abusers start to abuse others as adolescents – at a time when they haven't even reached their full maturity. The reasons why someone becomes abusive towards others are still to be fully researched.

However, research involving the use of lie detectors has revealed an interesting contradiction, and something that might help eventually to uncover what it is that makes a person become abusive.

In a study of adolescent boys who had sexually abused others, it was found that over 60% claimed to have been abused themselves. However, when asked again in a lie detector test, this number dropped to around 30%.

There has been a widely held view that all people, mostly males, who sexually abuse others have themselves been abused. This has done a huge disservice to the vast majority of male survivors of childhood sexual abuse who do not go on to abuse others.

It has placed barriers in the way of male survivors accessing services, making them afraid that they will be judged to be abusive themselves if they tell anyone.

It has also led to fathers who are survivors feeling afraid to show their own children the love and affection they feel through cuddling and hugging.

Until we can extend our knowledge of why someone becomes abusive, people in society have to take responsibility for protecting those who cannot protect themselves. Unfortunately, there is a struggle to match resources with the need revealed by the demand for support from survivors. We are left with a different battle. Education.

We need to teach all adults about their responsibilities towards children. We need to teach people to be aware of the need to protect children and vulnerable adults. We need to teach people not to be abusers. We need to teach everyone about how to avoid situations where people might take advantage of them, and we need to educate survivors to explain that you can grow and achieve in life, despite bad experiences.

We need to empower everyone not to accept abuse. We all need to feel safe in our lives. If we are not safe we cannot develop fully. This must come from empowering young people, so they feel confident talking to anyone who will listen.

Young people need to be able to say when they feel unsafe and uncomfortable. They need to be able to recognise when they are uncomfortable or unhappy in a given situation. Adults need to be able to respond to this emotional need. In the meantime, it is the adults in society who must take full responsibility for protecting the children and the vulnerable adults in society.

If you are concerned about anyone's behaviour towards children, or if you are worried about your own behaviour, then there is a child sexual abuse prevention campaign called Stop It Now!

Stop It Now! produces leaflets and booklets that help people to recognise potentially abusive behaviour in adults, children or young people. They have a confidential freephone helpline and a website:

0808 1000 900

www.stopitnow.org.uk

CHAPTER 4

STARTING YOUR JOURNEY TO HEALING

WHY DO YOU NEED A SUPPORT NETWORK?

Ask yourself what has helped you the most?

Starting your journey to healing

A support network is necessary because we are social beings and we have to interact with one another to develop. In order to learn we need to share our problems.

Who can you talk to?

In order to build a support system for yourself, you need to think about your relationships with your friends now. Who is it that you can talk to?

Who can you phone? Who can you text? At anytime?

You need to know they will listen and be interested in you. Who is it that you can you rely on to speak to if necessary in the middle of the night?

It might be a good idea to write down some of the people you know who you can call on in times of need.

What is it about those people that make them helpful? It might be that different individuals have different qualities that can be relied upon at different times.

Suggestion: write here the names of your supporters, their telephone numbers and why they may be of help to you?

_____

_____

_____

_____

_____

_____

_____

_____

_____

_____

_____

_____

Your support network might be drawn from your friends or family, or your partner. They might be people from a self-help group.

Or you might like to consider who, if you told them that you are a survivor, would be supportive once they knew.

Like many survivors, you may feel overwhelmed at the support friends will give when you do tell them that you have had negative experiences.

In time, you may be able to be part of someone else's support network.

Starting your journey to healing

If you have not managed to write down many names, then you might need to consider joining a support group. Or you might have to consider who among your friends you could tell.

It might be that you have not told your partner and you might consider doing so now.

If you do not yet feel comfortable in telling your partner or friends, then you could contact helplines.

There is a list of organisations at the back of this book where you can find support (page 323).

What helplines do you know? No one to call ? What's your favourite survivor website?

If you can't think of a friend, or don't feel able to talk to someone you know, the Samaritans provide confidential emotional support 24 hours a day to anyone who is going through a crisis:

08457 90 90 90

www.samaritans.org

Think about what you can do to start to build up your support network. You may be surprised to find that many of the people you already know would welcome a closer friendship.

SENSITIVITY TO THE HURT

The hurt child
(recognising the hurt child in you)

When a person is working with young people, they will recognise when they meet 'the angry, hurt, young person'. They may be behaving in an aggressive manner. The temptation for some people is to judge the behaviour of the child. Yet, if they knew what had been done to that child, they would be more understanding.

The key to understanding the behaviour is to discover what has happened to the child. Then this needs understanding. We might ask them the question, 'How might it be if all that had been done to that child had been done to you?' You would be amazed at someone else listening to your story and respecting your views.

Some survivors who have been harmed exhibit behaviour that can be classed as antisocial. They are often angry at what life has thrown at them. In a complex web of emotions they are seeking to make sense of it all. It may be that as a child a survivor can find common social interaction difficult.

Often there has been shouting and aggression for a long period of time, so that it has influenced that person in every aspect of who they appear to be.

This could be called damage. A hurt that has lingered has penetrated their personality. In education we say there is a child who has behavioural difficulties not a child who is bad.

Many survivors of childhood sexual abuse will recognise that their early years were often marked out by seemingly obvious signs of distress – truanting, bedwetting, night terrors that no-one seemed to notice or pay any attention to.

VALUABLE

There may have been times when you do not feel valuable. To become valuable you have to believe you're worth it. A person can only judge how valuable they are if they are able to understand themselves in the context of others.

You must believe that you are valuable.

Go and watch the film 'It's a Wonderful Life'. This film is about a man on the verge of suicide. An angel comes to show him how it would have been if he had never lived. At the end the main character is inspired and uplifted.

We all need to feel that 'feel good' factor, that somehow the world is a better place because we have lived in it.

Go for a swim – the sensation of water all around you is relaxing. Swimming is one of the best forms of exercise. There is a real healing sense in swimming because you can relax.

GROWING UP

Amber, Raoul and Niles had very different experiences. Psychologists talk about parents being 'good enough' to give their children the care and nurturing they need to grow into emotionally healthy adults. This is in recognition of the fact that it is impossible to be perfect at all times.

For Amber, her mother was able to give her good enough mothering and care for her to have an understanding of what it means to be loved and cared for. Even though she has been sexually abused, Amber has a solid foundation to build future relationships on. The fact that it did not protect her from the abuse is an indication of how difficult it can be to identify an abuser.

Unfortunately, for Raoul, his mother was herself abusive and Raoul needed to find someone else to provide the emotional stability that all children need. Thankfully, his grandmother lived close by, and although she may have been unable to show her daughter love, she was able to be kind towards Raoul. This provided him with enough emotional input for him to develop an awareness of what positive relationships can be like.

WHY DON'T YOU LOVE ME?

Conflicting emotions

When a child is abused by someone who is a parent or caring figure in their lives, they are faced with a terrible choice. They can choose to believe that the parent or carer is someone who is capable of causing them pain and hurt for no apparent reason. Or they can decide that actually the parent or carer has good reasons for hurting them – they must have been very naughty or bad to deserve being hurt.

Rational thinking tells us that is nonsense but in these difficult situations that can often appear to be the stark choice. Our inner child's emotions become very confused about what is happening.

An abuser may even use this idea of it being the child's fault to encourage a child to believe that the child is to blame for the abuse. 'Look what you've made me do', Amber's Uncle used to say.

For a child, their home is the whole world to them. To decide that their parent or someone close to the family is a negative, hurtful person means that their whole world can be negative and hurtful.

On the other hand, if the child believes that they are responsible for the abuse happening, by being naughty somehow, then this offers the chance for them to 'be good' and so stop the abuse. If they can only be as good as they can, then the abuse will not happen.

Of course, the abuse has nothing to do with whether a child is well behaved or not. In fact, children often express distress through misbehaving in some way.

Here you might like to make notes about your feelings about what you have just read

EASY MEDITATION EXERCISE

Many people try out meditation because they want to experience a feeling of peace. What they often find is that instead of their minds going clear, they find that thoughts push in and stop them from relaxing.

Try out this exercise. It is a really easy way of experiencing a feeling of meditation.

Make sure you won't be disturbed and sit comfortably. Then close your eyes and imagine that you are looking at a gently flickering candle.

As you breathe, concentrate on counting your breaths slowly in and out. One thousand, two thousand, three thousand, one thousand, two thousand, three thousand.

Counting gives your mind something else to concentrate on rather than any other worries. Don't worry if other thoughts come into your mind. Just continue counting slowly. You can sit still and count for several minutes. As you practice more, you will find it even easier. Some people get into the habit of meditating for regular periods during the week.

Meditation is about being still and getting grounded and in control. When things are getting really bad you might like to develop the practice of 'time out'. This means that you find a space at home that is for you. You might like there to be cushions and incense and candles. You might like to sit in a meditation posture or relax by lying down.

There you can have time to be calm and reflect on beautiful thoughts. This is not meditation strictly, but a soothing time for you. Take the phone off the hook. You might like to play a relaxation tape. They have ones with sounds of the sea, for example. If you seriously want to practice meditation you might want to join a group or at least read up on the activity.

RELATIONSHIP PATTERNS

It is a very frightening idea for a child to believe that their mother or father is abusive and they resist the idea by becoming very scared of losing their attachment to the parent. This can explain why even when a child has been very badly abused, they still feel love towards the parent and would not wish any harm to come to them.

Some people have called this 'doublespeak' – the ability to have two conflicting emotions about someone or something at the same time. You may both love and fear the abuser. You may detest the abusive behaviour, and yet still yearn for that parent to show you love and affection. Sometimes, a person can get into a pattern of relationships where they replay these feelings over and over again.

You may find yourself in unequal relationships where you have to strive to feel loved. You don't enjoy feeling this way, but it's a familiar feeling. If someone treats you kindly and respectfully, you may feel uncomfortable without knowing why.

It takes time and self-awareness to break free of this pattern but it can be done. Sometimes it can help to have couple-counselling so that these conflicts can be brought out into the open, and so there is the opportunity to develop a new pattern for the relationship.

Towards a positive future

You may feel that the harm that has been done to you in your life will have made you very unhappy and that this cannot change. What needs to happen is that you can somehow be encouraged to see that you can go forward.

A person who has been raped or abused needs to know that they can be healed. You can feel better. There is a positive future. It may take time, but progress is possible.

For each person, this journey is going to be different. For some it will be easier than others. In some people's lives, the anger and pain they have experienced is so profound that they are psychologically wounded.

Can we even dare to talk about healing the wounds? Yes. We believe it is possible to heal the wounds and the pain. In every case it is possible to live a more positive life.

We are dealing with trauma and moving beyond suffering and putting individual lives on an even keel.

Negative Self-Care

You may find it difficult to start to care for yourself, and you may have found some negative ways of caring for yourself in the past:

- ➢ Drinking too much?
- ➢ Over-eating?
- ➢ Under-eating
- ➢ Over-working?
- ➢ Self injury?
- ➢ Gambling?
- ➢ Drugs?
- ➢ Over-spending?
- ➢ Destructive relationships?
- ➢ Being angry?
- ➢ Maybe you have confused love with sex and chased love by having many sexual partners.

We don't really need to tell you that these are all negative ways of caring, but it can feel very harsh to finally admit that this is what you are doing.

For all the times you have kicked yourself and pulled yourself down, you're going to have to counteract that with a positive response.

That takes time and determination.

What we do believe in is people's amazing ability to use their potential to overcome and develop themselves beyond their perceived limitations.

Be honest - what are the negative ways you care for yourself?

_____

_____

_____

_____

Do you love yourself? Are you loveable? These are simple questions. But for many survivors, these are the most difficult questions of all. And if you don't love yourself, then how are you going to share love with someone else?

In a while Amber, Raoul and Niles will be talking about ways in which we can move towards loving ourselves, but in the meantime:

What are the good ways you care for yourself? Be as creative here as you can be!

_____

_____

_____

_____

_____

_____

Decide to smile. It doesn't cost anything at all. Even if you don't feel like smiling, if you make yourself smile you start to release chemicals in your body that will lift your mood. Look in the mirror and frown at yourself. Now smile at yourself until your eyes crinkle up. Which face do you want your friends and family to know?

POSITIVE

You need to be positive. Do you see the cup half full or half empty? To be positive all of the time may be impossible. Each day one sees or hears about misfortune. How easy it is to give up on people. Yet to see that tomorrow is another day is a real use of willpower. Perhaps we will have to will ourselves to be positive. How many people do you know who are negative?

What we need is the smile on a person's face. If we do not see this, then we should take the moment to put a smile on someone's face. People might say to you that whenever they see you, you are always smiling. This is vital. The ability to smile and sparkle with hope in difficult situations will help to uplift yourself and others. You might say it is wishful thinking, or simply being naïve, yet what is the alternative? To live your life in a negative light or to live seeking inspiration and raising hope in others?

'At first, I would have said that it was impossible to will myself to be positive. I just couldn't do it. Getting through every day felt like a battle. After a while though, I started to recognise where I could actually tell myself that I had to be positive and emphasise the good things in my life rather than the negative things. Sometimes it was easier to do this than others. Looking back over my journal could be helpful in the difficult times – it was a reminder that I had felt worse (and better).' Niles

Here you might like to write down a response to the questions that follow

What can you do today that is a positive act of nurturing yourself?

_____

_____

_____

What can you do this week that will help you feel good about yourself?

_____

_____

_____

What can you do to reward yourself for getting this far through the book?

_____

_____

_____

_____

Go out with friends. Invite a friend round. Ring a friend or email them. Write them a letter.

FEELINGS CHECK

If you do the same old things without making changes, then you will find the same old things happening again and again.

If you say, 'I never have time to do anything for myself'; this allows the same old feelings to stay with you.

If you say, 'What's the point?', you are denying yourself the opportunity of finding out about yourself.

Okay, we've come this far. We've also looked at some coping strategies for those times when we go over the top instead of reacting in a thoughtful and productive way, See the section on mood swings, page 52

Where is all this leading? Well, hopefully, what we're doing is interesting you in the possibility that you can actually change your life to make it more fulfilling and happy. It won't happen overnight, the foundations need to be solid and strong and these take time to build, but you have already started to build them. Now, let's ask you a crucial question:

What do you want to change in your life?

By starting to believe you can make changes you are making a real step towards a positive future.

Check it out: what do you want to change in your life?

Is it something you can change? (You can't change other people, only yourself)

_____

_____

_____

Is it a reasonable change? (Is it something that can happen? We haven't got the lottery numbers)

_____

_____

_____

What do you need to do to make the change?

_____

_____

_____

What will hinder you making the change?

_____

_____

_____

What will help you making the change?

_____

_____

_____

What can you do today towards this change?

_____

_____

_____

How will you know when you have made the change?

_____

_____

_____

HAVE I BEEN ABUSED?

Many people who experience an abusive incident are left feeling unsure of themselves and find it difficult to actually believe that they have been raped or abused. You might deny the experience to yourself, or you may refuse to believe that you have been affected by it.

Many survivors tell themselves that what they have been through is 'not so bad' as what has happened to lots of other people. You might feel that it will take up time at the support services that other people deserve more. You may feel that your friends and family don't want to hear about your troubles.

We believe that it is really important for someone who has been raped or sexually abused to know that it is not so much what has happened – the type of abuse, or the number of times someone has been abused - that causes the real emotional and psychological damage.

The real hurt to your inner child comes from the total loss of trust when you realise that your world has not been a safe place for you. Even that someone, who should have loved and protected you, has failed to be able to do that.

Join a natural voice choir – no experience necessary. Everyone has a voice that can be used to make beautiful sounds. There can also be a really enjoyable experience when a person is singing. That is why the great singers touch our hearts. The sound is their soul being expressed.

'There's something good about being able to sing out loud and clear. Maybe it's after all the years of silence.' Niles

LOSS OF TRUST

After such loss of trust and faith, all relationships that follow can feel tainted by this, and lifelong patterns of fear and mistrust of everyone can develop.

Maybe you will recognise where you have somehow punished the very people who have shown you the most love and affection, or where you have failed to ever believe that you can be loved and accepted for who you are.

The reason for this conflict is that it is your inner child's feelings that are reacting to what is happening. No matter what your mind might tell you, the feelings in your heart remain fearful and mistrusting no matter how much love someone may show you.

To start to heal, your inner child needs to start to feel loved and cared about. You need to start showing this love and care for yourself – even in the little ways our teddies suggest – so that you can start accepting it from others.

DEPENDABLE

We all need people to depend on. It is a wonderful quality to develop in yourself. People will come to rely on you and depend on your stability and personal integrity.

'I have learnt to allow my friends to support me. I do not pester them. I do depend on them for support. I know that they are there for me.' Raoul

---

Traumatic experiences may underlie lots of negative ways of behaving in life, towards others and towards ourselves – insecurity, jealousy, drug and alcohol misuse, unfaithfulness, and physical and verbal aggression – BUT that's not to say that it is an excuse for any of these reactions.

Starting your journey to healing

Understanding why you may have behaved in a negative way will help you to identify how you can change that behaviour.

Talk things through with a trusted friend, partner or counsellor. Make recovery a joint venture. How wonderful if you are able to make this journey with someone who is supportive.

Later on we look at the many different ways rape and sexual abuse can affect someone in their life. First we want you to take some time to think about how you believe your own life might have been affected. How would you want your life to be different?

How do you think your life has been affected?

_____

_____

_____

_____

_____

_____

_____

_____

_____

_____

_____

Thinking forward and seeing how things could be in the future, helps focus the mind onto the possibilities. You encourage your inner child to have hope. So, if you can imagine your life really improved, you are making an affirmation towards the real possibility of that happening in the future.

How do you want your life to be different?

_____

_____

_____

_____

_____

_____

_____

_____

_____

_____

_____

_____

_____

_____

_____

What is one thing that you can do today towards making your life how you want it to be?

_____

_____

_____

_____

_____

_____

_____

_____

_____

_____

_____

_____

_____

CHAPTER 5

LIFE PLANNING

In order to make a start towards healing, you will need to make some plans. You will need to make preparations and plans for the changes you want to make in your life. Here are some suggestions to help you start planning.

Amber and Raoul's life-plan journey

Here is a blueprint to explain to you what we are going to call 'forward thinking'. Life is not a rehearsal. When someone has experienced trauma, it is easy for time to slip by in a daze of pain, until they start to wonder where the years have gone. If you want something in life, then you need to plan for it.

So for example, let's imagine you want to have a plan for a journey sometime in the future. This journey is going to be a metaphor for your life plan.

Life planning

If you want an exciting, dynamic, unforgettable journey you will need to plan. In order for the journey to be successful and significant, you need to choose:

- The date that you will set off on the journey
- The destination: where do you want to get to?
- The necessary provisions that you will need on the way;
- The entertainment or amusements that you want to accompany you on your way
- Who you want to invite to accompany you on your journey?
- What to do if there are delays or setbacks?
- What will your ticket for the journey actually say?
- You will need to think about all the things that you also want to happen along the way

Obviously, if the journey isn't planned properly, it won't turn out the way you want it to.

Do you know where you want to go?

If the answer is no, then it doesn't matter which way you go, does it?

What would you like your life journey to be like?

_____

_____

_____

_____

_____

_____

_____

_____

_____

_____

_____

Let's make a comparison between our planned journey and our lives. If we don't plan into our lives some activities and events, including meeting people, then where will our interest and enthusiasm for life come from? This would appear to be perfectly obvious, but so many survivors become stuck, by expecting things to happen to them, rather than making things happen themselves.

But the really powerful thing here is imagining your journey, with all your planning, going as you intended it to be. Can you imagine that you can create the atmosphere in your mind, seeing you and your family thoroughly enjoying the journey to the places where you would like to go?

If you plan your journey by forward thinking you will have done all you can to make it match your expectations as you travel through life.

IT'S YOUR LIFE!

In order to choose which way you are going in life, you need to take a look at some of the possibilities that are open to you. Before you make your choices, consider them carefully. There must be aspects of your life that are not how you want them to be. This knowledge has led you wanting to find a resolution and healing.

Now, here is a chance for you to think about where you would like your life journey to take you. Start by giving yourself some quiet time, when you won't be disturbed, and ask yourself the following questions.

Where would you like your life journey to take you?

1.   **What do you want to happen in the next three months?**

        To yourself:

        To your relationships:

        At work/home:

2.   **What do you want to happen in the next six months:**

        To yourself:

        To your relationships:

        At work/home:

3.   What is important for you in the next year?

To yourself:

To your relationships:

At work/home:

4.   What are the most important things for you in the next five years?

To yourself:

To your relationships:

To work/home:

5.   When you look back over your life journey, what would you like to think has happened?

To yourself:

To your relationships:

To work/home:

Life planning

Looking ahead like this allows you to have a perspective on your life that many survivors don't often seek out. It can identify what really is most important for you, whether this is in family, friendships, relationships or work.

Are the most important things at six months the same as they are for five years' time? What about the most important things for your whole lifetime?

What do you want to be able to look back on as your achievements in life?

Thinking about your life in this way can be very daunting, and even scary if you aren't used to making choices or planning. Why not come back to this section later on and see if your answers are still the same? If they're different, in what ways are they different and why do you think that might be?

As you continue on the process of healing, be constantly aware of the things that you want to change in your life and how you might start to build those changes.

 **Make time for yourself alone to do something that you enjoy, for no other reason than that you enjoy it. What would you choose your hobby to be? Do you want something quiet and relaxing like fishing or painting, or something invigorating and exciting like rallying or gym classes?**

What do you want to be able to look back on as your achievements in life?

_____

_____

_____

_____

_____

_____

_____

_____

_____

_____

_____

_____

_____

_____

_____

Obviously, you cannot plan for every event that could happen, but what this is allowing you to do is to identify with something that might happen in the future. It gives you something to aim for, and it does help to have some structure.

You will find that the more precise your planning the more likely you are to be satisfied that it turned out as near to your expectations as possible.

Life planning

So, what will happen if you apply planning to your relationships? First of all, you could decide what you would like to have in your relationships. Maybe something like:

- ➢ Mutual respect
- ➢ Love for one another
- ➢ Co-operation between each other
- ➢ Developing and encouraging confidence in each other
- ➢ Being able to trust each other
- ➢ Appreciation of others

 *Planning for your relationships*

What does 'mutual respect' mean to you?
_____
_____
_____

What does 'love' mean to you?
_____
_____
_____

What are the ways you can co-operate with others?
_____
_____
_____

How do you develop and encourage confidence in others?

_____

_____

_____

How does it feel to trust someone?

_____

_____

_____

How do you show your appreciation for someone?

_____

_____

_____

Maybe you have identified something that needs to be different in your relationships?

Listen to what your inner wisdom is telling you.

YOUR RELATIONSHIPS BLUEPRINT

What needs to change? (Remember, you can't change other people, you can only change yourself. BUT, if your responses to others change from being suspicious to being open, then you will notice a change in how other people respond to you.)

What will make you feel comfortable, safe, secure, and happy in your relationships? As you write this down, you will be putting down signposts on the road that are going to help you improve your relationships

_____

_____

_____

_____

_____

_____

_____

_____

Each person's blueprint for building relationships is going to be entirely different. The steps might be quite long or short to get to your destination.

It is the process of identifying some markers for your plan that will help you to get to where you want to be.

So, for example, if communication is an issue, what are you going to suggest is the appropriate way forward to help with communication? Will it be simply a matter of finding some time together, other than writing messages or texting each other? Do you need more time together alone, privacy from distractions? Maybe you need heart-to-heart conversations, telling each other what you really feel as opposed to what you think they would like to hear.

The wizards know that you will already be aware of what isn't working properly in your relationships. Take some time now to write down what you want to begin to heal in your relationships.

 *What do you want to begin to heal in your relationships?*

_____

_____

_____

_____

_____

_____

_____

FINDING SOLUTIONS

Now, somebody once said that if you think out your problem clearly, you will know deep down how you will go about fixing it. If that is true, and you're honest with yourself, then you will know the possible solutions to the problems you are facing.

The biggest hurdle is for you to personally choose how you are going to make those first steps towards the goal that you have chosen for yourself.

It might be that you're not ready to think about planning your entire future life. But whether you are thinking of short-term or long-term goals, we are offering suggestions here, which can apply to any situation.

If one of your goals is to be healthier, then you need to ask yourself how you are going to go about it. Is there one thing you can change that will help you?

You will be taking small steps towards focusing your life in a more positive way.

ONE STEP AT A TIME

If you think of that first step, of what you need to put in place, to start you on the way to making progress, you've got to find the confidence within yourself to believe that you can do it!

It might be that you have to learn a skill that you don't have yet. It might be that you've got to pick up the 'phone and arrange to get on that course. Or you've got to go and talk to somebody about how you are feeling.

Or you've got to challenge someone close, to say, 'This is where I would like us to be going in our relationship.'

You might now gain the confidence to say to yourself, 'This is what I have to do to make a better tomorrow.' And as you lay down those first few steps as stages on the way to your goal, you've got a far better chance of achieving your dreams than if you do not plan.

FUTURE PLANNING

Now think back to the plan for your life - you could plan ahead for the next day, or could you plan for longer-term events. What is the difference? The real difference is the scale of the vision, the kind of detail you would want to include in your plan.

We want to encourage in you the belief that you can have the confidence and that you could plan ahead. Why would you want to do this? Because if your heart is set on a sincere belief that you can do it, then this can motivate you to do it. Then all your friends will have the chance to share in your vision. Get them on board with your planning.

So, if your ambition for your relationships included other members of your family, like how you are going to have more successful relationships with your children, your in-laws, and colleagues at work, you will need to make a few major staging posts for your plan.

Life planning

What would you like your life journey to be like?

Identify what isn't working at the moment.

Imagine how you would like the things to be.

Work out how you will know when you have achieved your goals.

Decide on three things you can do today towards your life journey.

Work out a back-up plan for if things don't quite work out how you thought they would.

Be realistic. Nobody's perfect, and you may need to be patient to see the results of your efforts.

I FEEL GOOD WHEN...

It may help to remind yourself of things that help you to feel good about yourself.

Feelings check

Things to feel good about yourself

> ➤ I feel good about myself when ...
>
> ➤ I feel content when ...
>
> ➤ I feel satisfied when ...
>
> ➤ I like myself when ...
>
> ➤ I am glad when I ...
>
> ➤ I have a feeling of accomplishment when I ...
>
> ➤ This will be a success for me because I will plan ...
>
> ➤ When someone says something positive about me I feel ...
>
> ➤ I have the potential to ...
>
> ➤ I am pleased when ...
>
> ➤ I feel proud when ...
>
> ➤ People like me when I ...
>
> ➤ I am getting better at ...
>
> ➤ People admire me for ...
>
> ➤ I am a good friend when ...

IS HEALING POSSIBLE?

In many cases, because of your experiences, you might feel that healing is impossible. It's generally easier to understand that the body can heal, but not so easy to understand how the mind can be healed.

What does healing mean? Firstly let us say healing is a positive act. There are many survivors who will at some time feel so bad that they don't want to know about healing, let alone believe it can happen.

To begin psychological and emotional healing, you have to make the decision to move towards it. This means accepting that there is a personal responsibility in identifying the changes and understanding needed for healing to take place, and then being prepared to put in the effort to achieve it.

First of all, you have to recognise that all the emotional and psychological pain from your experiences has gone inside your mind to the inner child.

You think negative things about yourself and these thoughts colour how you behave. As your thoughts go round and round, focusing on negative beliefs about yourself, the worse you feel and your mind becomes more and more depressed. This process is not difficult to understand. Here it is in a nutshell: it takes more energy to think sad thoughts than to think positive ones.

HEALING MYSELF

The first step towards healing is to understand the emotions of the past.

Question: Can I heal myself?

Yes you can. What is more, to regain control of your life you need to do it. Here we will tell you some of the ways that you might go about healing yourself.

The first thing you need to know is that self-healing can be done alone. This is not to devalue self-help groups. What we are saying is that the wish to heal has to come from the person who needs the healing. No amount of therapy or support will help you if you do not want to be healed.

Some people believe that if they think about the trauma it will make the effect on them worse, and they try to ignore their feelings. This can work for a while, even for years, but eventually for many people the memories of being abused do not fade away, but fester and cause ongoing pain. The inner child continues to suffer. If you do not repair the emotional and psychological damage done to you, then the effects can be physical and long term.

SETBACKS

People can live their lives, but have had their inner potential cut off or destroyed as a result of abuse. People can even die early as a result of sexual or emotional abuse.

You ask, 'How can that be?'

A person is an emotional being. Intense suffering has a physical effect on the body that can be simply described as stress. Stress is the effect trauma records on a person's physical and psychological health.

Trauma acts on a person in a physical way. Blood pressure increases, cholesterol levels are increased and the body becomes exhausted by being permanently switched onto 'red alert'. Nerves become shattered, and anxiety and depression are common.

We have to take seriously the fact that how we think is going to influence how we feel about ourselves. If someone thinks they are useless then they do not give themselves permission to be anything else. If they think they can't, then they don't give themselves the chance to try.

There will inevitably be dark days. No one is denying that. What has to happen is that you have to will yourself to get back on top. If you are constantly thinking negative thoughts then you do not allow yourself the opportunity for positive thoughts to come in.

PATIENCE

It is not going to happen overnight. Everyone recognises that time is required to take on new ideas. If you think carefully about some of the steps suggested in this programme and apply a few of the ideas then you will make progress. It will need patience. We are all different and think differently.

MAKING CHANGE HAPPEN

If you have spent some time feeling down, then your thoughts are likely to be more negative than positive. You may even pick up on negative ideas more quickly than positive ideas. You may be so used to telling yourself that you aren't good enough or that you can't do something, that you have lost the ability to believe anything else. This is like punishing your inner child.

This is where you have to give yourself a break. If you need a reminder, look back at the section on *Human Rights (page 56)*. You deserve the same chances and opportunities as everyone else. If you have made any mistakes, then we all have a right to learn from past mistakes.

While you are still developing trust in yourself, it's really important to be listening out for your own self-criticism. Every time you catch yourself thinking something negative about yourself, think STOP! Remember you are talking to your inner child. Would you constantly tell a child it was naughty or bad? If you had a friend who was being self-critical, you would surely tell them not to be so harsh with themselves, and then remind them of all their positive qualities and achievements. This is what you need to do for yourself.

ENTHUSIASTIC

You are approaching becoming the person you would like to be because you are committed and enthusiastic in your endeavour.

In order to heal yourself, you have to believe you are worth it!

You can talk yourself down with negative thoughts so quickly that nothing will change. You have to believe that you can change, and remember that the change has to occur inside of you.

 *Here are some questions to ask yourself*

How do you respect yourself?

_____

_____

_____

_____

How do you care for yourself?

_____

_____

_____

_____

_____

Write down some of the ways you care for yourself

How do you develop trust in yourself?

What kind of a person do you want to be?

What things do you imagine will be happening when you start to feel happy?

How do you see yourself in the future?

Some people find gardening therapeutic. If you do not have a garden, plant a window box. If you only have a flat then make an indoor garden. There are jars or planters for indoor plants. Watch the plants and seeds grow. Plant some herbs for your kitchen windowsill. Enjoy watching your favourite herbs growing ready to be used in your meals. Of course, some people do not enjoy gardening. Yet, it is still important to have some connection to living things. One suggestion is buy bamboo that can be kept just in water.

When we wrote this section we were reminded of an old Chinese Proverb:

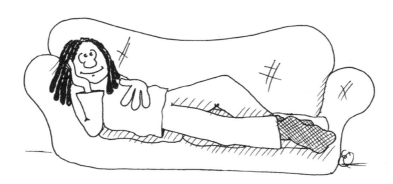

'Happiness is like a butterfly. Seek it and it will elude you. Turn your mind to other things and it comes and sits happily on your shoulder.'

This saying is very true. Seeking happiness will be difficult.

But, guess what?

You have to give yourself permission to feel good about yourself.

It sounds ridiculous, but it is true. You need to believe that someone, namely you, is giving you permission to take control and make decisions for yourself. If you can't see a positive future then you have to make it happen.

If you visualise yourself in the future managing to get back on track, then this can be a powerful tool towards healing.

Life planning

CHAPTER 6

YOUNG SURVIVORS

What happens to young survivors?

This section is here for those who have not spoken up and need the encouragement to do so. We are talking to a young survivor, or indeed an older survivor who was abused as a child and has never spoken out. They are going to have to speak out now for the child within themselves who never told anyone.

We know that these are common things for survivors to think about themselves and about what has happened to them:

'No one will believe me'

> You will be believed. If the first person you tell does not take any action, then tell someone else. Do not get brushed away, keep talking until someone pays attention.

Young survivors

'I am the only one this has happened to'

> The statistics are proof that this isn't so. It is natural to feel this way, but you are not alone in having traumatic experiences.

'My Dad said he would kill me'

> It's understandable to be frightened when you have been threatened. But help and protection is there for you. It is your right to be protected.

'Will I be put in prison?'

> No! You have done nothing wrong, but you might have been lied to and told this would happen.

'Am I to blame?'

> It is never the child's fault.

You have a right to be heard

If someone is abusing you, they may be abusing others. You must get help. If you have been abused in the past, it will help to be able to talk about it. You must know it is not your fault.

The first step in this case is to find an adult you trust who you can tell. The best person to speak to in school is the chosen teacher who is responsible for child protection. If you feel you cannot talk to them, then you should talk to any teacher who you feel is sympathetic. The teacher will listen. They will have to take immediate steps to ensure your safety.

What this may mean is that if the person who is abusing you is someone in the family home, then they may be asked to leave the home until investigations have been carried out.

This can appear to be very frightening. You may feel that you have even less control over what is happening than you had before you told anyone. This is difficult, but the abuse will hopefully stop.

It might mean that you could be removed from the home and placed in foster care for your own safety until after any investigations. This will only happen in the most extreme cases. If the person who was abusing you was a family member, then they may be removed from the home or asked to leave.

Usually, social services do all they can to keep a family together. This can be a very good thing since it allows the family to pull together. However, if the abuse continues, you must speak out. It is your right to be safe. Although it might be difficult for you right now, you need to be safe.

Want to tell, but worried what will happen

In the most serious cases, then the police will be immediately involved and the abuser might be arrested. If this happens, you will be assigned a social worker who will support you through any possible court case.

Medical examinations may be needed, and the police may want a statement to be made.

If the Crown Prosecution Service decides to take action, then there are Home Office Guidelines set out for the types of support and therapy that a young person may have before the case is heard. The guidelines must be followed carefully so that the evidence for the court case is not jeopardised.

Some young people are very determined that they want court action to be taken. Others do not wish this to happen at all. You need to know that you can choose what happens and that there is support available for you as a witness if you decide to make a full statement to the police.

If you want to find a way to stop the abuse, but are frightened of telling anyone because the police will be involved, then you could contact Childline or the NSPCC helpline. The number is free and will not show up on a telephone bill. They will be allow you to talk through your fears and concerns and will support you in making choices that will help you to find a way through what is happening.

Childline

0800 11 11

NSPCC Helpline

0808 100 25 24

Confusion as to what is happening

A child who is not informed about sex or understands very little about the body, would have every right to feel confused or disturbed. Some adults who are abused do not cope well. It must be horrific for a child. The correct philosophy is that a child will slowly grow into a mature understanding of their body and other people's. Then they will learn how sex works. If an inappropriate act occurs at a young age the trauma will affect them in many ways. The stress may enter their inner self.

It may be that a child knows what took place is wrong. They may never speak about it. They may not remember it clearly. Not all children will behave in the same way. There is no fixed explanation of the behaviour that may follow.

Pornographic images

Children do not have the emotional development to fully understand pornographic material. They have the right to be innocent of such things.

Young children are generally bemused by pornographic images. They don't really understand the meaning of the images they are looking at. Children will often know enough that the images are not something they should talk about to others, sensing or being told that they must keep quiet, but they are not physically or emotionally ready to fully comprehend their meaning. Pornography may then have a different meaning for that child, and be used by them to masturbate or involve other children in sexual activity.

The effect of sexual abuse on a child

When a child is sexually abused, their bodies respond to sexual stimulation as all human bodies do. This results in their behaviour becoming sexualised, as they become aware of their own bodies in a sexual way.

Children have the right not to be abused

Children have a natural, biological rate at which they develop, and at which their bodies and minds mature to the point where they are ready to enter into an intimate and sexual relationship with a partner of their choice.

Legally, the age at which someone is deemed to be mature enough to enter into a sexual relationship is sixteen years of age. There are very good reasons why an age limit is imposed on sexual activity. This is because sexual activity is not an isolated act in itself, it is linked to emotional development. Young people who engage in sexual activity at a very early age are not mature enough to handle these intense relationships.

Taking indecent photographs

Children whose behaviour becomes sexualised as a result of abuse, may not regard sex as a loving, intimate and tender act to share with a respected, loved and valued partner. Rather they may see it as something that is 'done to' someone as part of a power dynamic, divorced from tender and caring emotions.

Children may also confuse sex and love, and believe that by engaging in sexual activity they are expressing or seeking love. Many survivors, particularly male survivors, will say that they have had lots of sex with many different partners, but never actually 'made love' to a partner. They feel this difference as a great loss in their lives, although they may struggle to change this.

There have been cases where children find their parents' porn magazines, this is not the same as a person showing porn to a child and seeing their reaction. Pornography is often used by a paedophile to accustom a child to sexual activity.

Niles comments about how Father Bernard used magazines to initiate sexual activity.

'I felt really grown up when I looked at the magazines he showed me. I felt like it was a special privilege just for me. Then he started asking me if I was turned on, or if I had a hard on. I was just seven years old.' Niles

Pornography is being used here by an abuser to groom the child by pushing the boundaries of acceptability. The child may be too embarrassed to say anything, or they may feel like they are being treated as a grown-up, and therefore not want to say anything.

Either way, once the boundaries have been pushed, it becomes easier for an abuser to push them further. The pornography may then be used to introduce sexual activity. The child may even feel that they are somehow to blame because they did not say anything when the first incident happened. An abuser may use this knowledge against the child to keep them from seeking help.

In every case of child pornography, children have done, maybe without full awareness and often under duress, what was asked of them. Paedophiles may also use the pictures as trophies and reminders of the abuse.

In many cases, the children are too young to even understand what taking a photograph means. Often drugs or alcohol are used to make a child compliant.

Paedophiles may take a photograph of a child they are abusing and later use the pictures as part of their masturbation fantasies. The photographs may also be used by a paedophile in the lead-up to them abusing a child.

There are photographs that were taken long ago that are still available. For the person concerned this is a source of trauma and distress that they have no control over. It might be that the survivor feels that the existence of these photographs is like the act of abuse is being repeated.

The police make strenuous efforts to trace the children in the images that they find using facial mapping techniques, but they are overwhelmed with the sheer number of children involved and progress is slow.

The Internet

The Internet has led to pornographic material of all kinds being much more readily available than it ever was. Unfortunately, this has also meant that child pornography has become a multi-billion dollar industry.

On every Internet connected PC pornographic images are now only a few mouse-clicks away. Sometimes pornography is placed under headings that seem totally unconnected.

What you can do

At the moment, the law is structured in a way that means someone can own many thousands of images and yet court action will only result in a community service order. This is because of the way pornographic images are graded in severity. Some people will deliberately store only low-grade images so that if they are caught they will not receive a prison sentence.

If you know that pornographic images of you are still in existence, you may fear that the images are still being used. You may feel devastated to think that the images may have been shared with others or be available on the Internet.

Joining a campaign or local support group will help you to feel that you have taken control and are actively fighting the use of pornographic images of children.

Look after your own inner child

There is no easy solution to offer you that will take away the pain of this knowledge.

It may help if you can find a photograph of yourself as a child to remind you of how helpless you were then. You were innocent and needed protection, not abuse. You had no power to stop adults abusing you when you were a child. What you do now is to protect and comfort your inner child from the pain and grief of what happened.

You could keep the photograph with your journal or in your mood box as a reminder that it is your inner child that needs to be comforted and to feel loved.

> ➤ How would you comfort a distressed child?
>
> ➤ What would you say to a child that had been abused?
>
> ➤ What do you need to tell your own inner child?

What do you need to tell your own inner child about what has happened to you?

_____

_____

_____

_____

_____

_____

_____

_____

_____

_____

_____

_____

_____

_____

_____

_____

CHAPTER 7

SURVIVORS AS PARENTS

For any parent to find out that their child has been abused is a devastating shock.

For a parent who has been abused themselves, then there may be the additional burden of knowing what the impact has been on their own life and the potential impact on their own child.

Parents seek to protect their children. To discover that your child has been harmed can be very frightening. The depth and range of your feelings may be overwhelming:

➢ Your initial reaction may be shock and disbelief

➢ You may find it difficult to believe that your child has been abused. It is common to deny that anything can have happened. Parents may even deny that their child has been affected by the abuse

➢ Sometimes children can appear not to have been affected by trauma, seeming to carry on as normal. This can be very misleading, since the child is actually hiding their emotions. The effects do not disappear, they return later with full force to cause havoc with a child's self-esteem and integrity

139

Survivors as parents

➢ You may feel angry at what has happened, and have no way of releasing that anger

➢ You may have feelings of being inadequate as a parent, and that there is nothing you can do to help

➢ You may feel guilty that your child has been abused, believing that you failed to protect them

➢ It may be that the person who has abused your child also abused you. It is not uncommon for family members to abuse different generations of children in the same family. You may have believed that what happened to you was a mistake, or that the abuser would not behave like that again

➢ You may even have been persuaded to believe that your relationship with an abuser was 'special' and not something that could happen to any other child in the family. It is understandable that you will feel guilt in this case, but it is vital that you take steps to follow your own healing journey

➢ You may worry that your child will never recover

Some parents feel that they must put their child before themselves. They might think that support for themselves will just take their time away from the child.

You may not want to think about your own experiences, but in order to support your child you need to feel strong and believe in yourself.

It is not selfish to care for yourself at this time. It will ensure that you can help your child in the best way possible.

Do not blame yourself for someone else's actions. The person who abused your child is the one at fault.

Children can't always speak out

It is perfectly natural for any parent in this situation to have strong emotions and to express them, but they should be careful in how they are expressed around the child. A child may pick up on the anger and shock around them, and interpret it as meaning that they have done something wrong. The atmosphere at home will also be disrupted. Staying calm and keeping to routines will help everyone to find their way through the trauma.

Many survivors are extremely protective towards their children. They often make sure that children know about safe touching and good or bad secrets. Often, they are very careful in how they cuddle and hold their children, and watchful of how others behave towards them.

It can therefore be a tremendous shock if their child discloses that they have been abused.

Many parents who are survivors punish themselves for not noticing that their child was being hurt. You need to remind yourself that children can often feel confused about what is happening, and may be too young to have the awareness that they can tell someone.

You may have told yourself that you would never allow a child of your own to be hurt in the same way you were yourself and feel angry with yourself for not being able to protect your child. As a survivor yourself, you may have done all you can to teach your child about abuse. The fact that your child has not told you when abuse happened does not mean that you have not been a protective parent. What it tells us all is that sexual abuse is a damaging experience that can leave children too frightened or confused to tell anyone – even loving parents.

Children may be told that they will be put into care, or that their family will be split up. They may be threatened with violence if they tell anyone. Do not feel that it is your failure if your own child is abused. It is the fault of the person who has abused them. Remember that the hurt you feel is going straight to your own inner child and bringing back all your own memories as well.

141

How your child might react

- ➢ Children may become withdrawn, or start to behave in ways associated with a younger age

- ➢ They may have temper tantrums

- ➢ They may lose or gain weight

- ➢ Younger children may complain of stomach pains

- ➢ They may have mood swings

- ➢ They may suffer from flashbacks

- ➢ They may feel lonely and isolated from family and friends

- ➢ Struggling to concentrate on a task

- ➢ Angry at parents and others

- ➢ Feeling dirty in themselves. This can be difficult when the young person is at the height of puberty

- ➢ Stealing from home and shops

- ➢ Distrust of adults, including parents

- ➢ Lying to parents and carers

- ➢ Self-injury, using a knife, compass point, razor blade and cutting themselves in a pattern, often systematically on their arms, burning, pulling hair, scratching, pinching. Even very young children may start to self-injure. It may be that younger children have not developed any alternative coping strategies for the intense and difficult emotions they are feeling and their distress is turned in on themselves

- ➢ Self hate

➤ Drug and alcohol abuse, including solvents glue and aerosol cans sprayed into the mouth

➤ A consequence can be playing truant. They might want to avoid PE because they don't want to take off their clothes or let others see their injuries. If they are self-injuring, they will not want others to see the wounds. (School may be the last place they want to be. In school you have to take responsibility, so running away might seem a logical way to deal with their problems)

➤ Finally, there may be none of the above. There may be a determined attitude to succeed in all they do. Becoming a perfectionist is like trying to have control over something

WHAT YOU CAN DO TO HELP

Most parents often feel helpless and powerless to support their child through the aftermath of sexual abuse. As a survivor, your own responses may be so strong; you may feel you have little to offer. You may even underestimate what you can do that will help your child.

No-pressure listening

Often the most supportive thing you can do is to be there to listen whenever your child wants to talk to you. There should not be any pressure on a child to talk about their experiences or how they are feeling, but they do need permission to talk when they do choose to. If you find your own emotions difficult to cope with, keep grounding yourself and remember that your child has a very precious resource in you – a loving and caring parent who believes them.

Honest answers

Your child may have many difficult questions about what has happened. Answering honestly will build up your child's trust and belief in you as their parent. Respect your child's need to know about what has happened to them. Children may have questions for which there are no straightforward answers – 'Why did it happen to me?' or 'What did they do that for?' are questions that no one may have the answer to. If there are no simple answers, then children deserve to know that as well. However, what your child needs to know most of all is that they have not done anything to cause the abuse to happen to them.

Constant reassurance

Children need constant reassurance that they are not to blame. They also need to be reassured that they have done the right thing in speaking out to you about the abuse. A child may have been threatened with physical violence against themselves or other members of their family, and may need to be reassured that they have done well to speak out about the abuse.

ACKNOWLEDGE

We must acknowledge what has happened. You have to accept and then say, 'Yes I know what happened was bad, but that does not mean I cannot go on to face a better tomorrow.'

'I think this is one of the hardest things to do. I found it really challenging to admit to myself that my childhood had been so awful. I wanted to be like everyone else and have happy memories to look back on. What I can take comfort in is that I know my own children have had a very different childhood to mine. They know I love them to bits. I have to stop myself spoiling them.' Raoul

Your own children can enjoy a happy childhood

Children need to have their feelings acknowledged, and may not have language skills to talk about their emotions. However, if they still go on to express their feelings in a negative way, by taking it out on others or being destructive, then they should still be disciplined in a structured and calm way.

If a child is very aggressive or destructive, then time out in another room for ten minutes will allow them time to cool down enough for them to be able to listen to what you want to say. When a child has a tantrum, it takes at least ten minutes, and often up to twenty minutes, for them to start to calm down sufficiently to be reasoned with.

CAPABLE

You have to develop a sense of capability. We are all much more capable than we realise. We have to just be open to that possibility.

'I felt so out of control at times, I wouldn't have said I was capable of doing anything worthwhile. It took time for me to start to calm my attitude down to the level where I could feel that I was behaving in a responsible way. After that I slowly started to feel that I was making progress: I was actually capable of making decisions and choosing what I did. That felt fantastic.' Raoul

---

What are some of the ways that show you have taken control and are capable of achieving what you want?

_____

_____

_____

_____

_____

_____

_____

_____

EDUCATING OUR CHILDREN

All children need to be educated about their personal space. They need to know that they have the right to their personal and inner dignity. They need to know they will be listened to if they need to talk to someone.

All parents should be helping children protect themselves by educating them about expectations. For example, they need to know if someone is taking advantage of them.

Parents advise about not talking to strangers, but it is often someone who is known to the child and the family who is abusive. What can help is if parents encourage children to be aware that they have the right to respect their own personal space. Children from a very young age can understand about personal space. Parents can teach children that it is their right to retain their self-respect. If this is done then it can be a strength in their upbringing.

Take some time out to spend with your family. Watch a fun movie together with your children. Join a video rental store. This will give you an opportunity to select more interesting films. Watching films is an emotional exercise. You can be involved in the process of empathy for the characters and this can't be a bad thing. Some films can be inspirational, like Whale Rider or Rabbit Proof Fence. Talk to your child about the film and how they feel about the characters.

If, for any reason, someone violates their personal space, the child will feel more confident to tell someone that it has happened. However, parents still need to be aware that children can be vulnerable to having their feelings manipulated by an older person.

The child will have to understand emotionally if abuse is occurring. It may shock some people to think that we need to educate in this way. We accept that our children will learn about other things that we might not feel are socially acceptable. They also need to be encouraged to understand their feelings. We need to be doing more towards work with boys to help them. So many problems arise because of a lack of an emotional education.

Many boys, for example, suffer from low expectations of themselves and are unable to express their emotions. If they are harmed in any way, then they can be even less able to articulate their feelings, and this can lead to frustration and depression.

We also need to recognise that children also act out of a sense of duty to protect vulnerable parents. A child who feels they cannot tell to spare their parents distress, may keep quiet. They may bear a secret for years. We do not always fully understand the burden a child may be carrying. If parents, thought about this would they not deal with their children in a different way?

It is interesting when discussing with children some basic boundaries, that we find out that they implicitly trust adults. Many children when growing up will cross boundaries because of their lack of social awareness.

Acceptable & unacceptable boundaries

> ➤ I have the right to go to the bathroom alone
> ➤ I have the right not to be touched inappropriately in any situation when I am changing my clothes
> ➤ I have the right not to be grabbed and touched if I don't want it
> ➤ I have the right to be alone in my bedroom
> ➤ I have the right to privacy
> ➤ I have the right to speak up if I feel someone has treated me unfairly

If given opportunity to talk about risks, children are capable of making wise decisions. However, without that opportunity, many children will cross even basic boundaries. Here are a few basic boundaries that children often cross.

> ➤ Some children go out and not tell their parents where they are going
> ➤ Some children will go and play on railway tracks
> ➤ Some young people see teachers out of school in their homes
> ➤ Some children put themselves at risk by getting into a stranger's car
> ➤ Some young people meet strangers for arranged sex via the Internet

What memories do you want your loved ones to have about your family life?

_____

_____

_____

_____

_____

_____

_____

_____

_____

_____

_____

_____

_____

_____

_____

CHAPTER 8

POSSIBLE CONSEQUENCES OF RAPE AND SEXUAL ABUSE

You have reached the most difficult part of the book. It is vital that you are feeling grounded when reading this section. Choose when and where you read through this section and make sure you feel grounded before you start.

In practical terms, we're reminding you to take care of yourself and we know we're stating the obvious: if you aren't eating properly or getting restful sleep, then your mood will be easily lowered.

If you can have someone to talk to about any of the themes in this chapter then please do so.

If you do find this section tough going, then please give yourself a break.

When you have survived rape or sexual abuse, you may feel that there is no one out there who can know how you feel. And in one sense you're right. No two people can ever share exactly the same experiences, and not everyone will experience the same emotional and physical responses. Yet there are similarities in how people respond to trauma. These experiences are described very briefly here in order to help show where people are coming from.

Possible consequences of rape and sexual abuse

It can be very daunting and frightening to look at the range, complexity and severity of possible responses, and yet we feel this is important in order to help you identify how someone's life and wellbeing can be affected by trauma.

Remember, not all survivors will experience all or even any of these responses.

Some survivors can feel that their experience has marked them out as damaged and that this has a permanent effect. What we want to do is encourage you to keep grounded and remember that you are not alone.

Do take the time now to keep positive and be encouraged to know that others have been there and have survived. These responses are normal human responses to trauma and do not mean that someone is less able to cope or weak.

Emotional trauma (like being involved in a disaster or a parent dying early), physical abuse and emotional abuse, can all leave similar patterns of effects and responses.

Reacting to trauma

It is important to remember that everyone has naturally different levels of ability in coping with trauma. Some people will feel very traumatised by being shown pornographic images. Others will say that an abuser 'only' used to touch them. There are no rules that govern how someone should react to trauma. You are not weaker or stronger depending on how you react, and neither does your reaction reflect on your character. You must believe this.

What matters is recognising what the impact has been, because then you can start to develop new ways of coping. Researchers are now beginning to piece together the full picture of the potential and possible impact on someone's health and life situation:

➢ Emotional and psychological well-being
➢ Physical health
➢ Mental health
➢ Self-belief
➢ Negative coping strategies

We are going to briefly look at all of these areas, and offer some positive suggestions for coping with some of these effects.

However, some of the conditions linked to the impact of sexual violence require specialist support and sometimes medical intervention.

The knowledge gained from recent research is allowing medical and counselling services to start to develop more appropriate ways of supporting survivors. However, there are still large areas of the country where there is little structured support, and even less awareness of just how someone's physical, mental, emotional and general life can be affected by rape and sexual abuse.

What you might have to do is to raise the awareness of your counsellor, GP or psychiatrist to these new research findings.

If you feel you suffer from a condition that you believe is linked to an abusive experience, then we strongly suggest that you talk to your doctor or counsellor about gaining the most appropriate support and treatment.

We don't want to suggest that it is inevitable that a survivor will experience any or all of these possible effects.

EMOTIONAL AND PSYCHOLOGICAL WELLBEING

There are many survivors who find their own ways of coping and understanding their experiences, and who go on to lead fulfilling and positive lives.

But there are also many survivors who suffer from the after effects of sexual violence unaware that they are suffering from conditions linked to a human body's normal response to trauma.

There are also many survivors who experience deeply distressing emotional responses to sexual violence, with disabling levels of guilt and shame around their experiences that lead them into negative ways of coping.

However, we want to tell you that healing is possible, and recognising where the hurt is coming from is the beginning of the healing process. This is a positive step.

The emotional impact of rape and sexual abuse may be something that is immediately obvious or, quite often, something that appears over time.

The impact of trauma leaves a strong and lasting impression on someone's mind that can come out in flashbacks, nightmares and chronic anxiety levels.

Flashbacks

Flashbacks can involve any or all of the senses in any combination. This means that someone may fully re-experience a traumatic event – sounds, smells, sights, emotions, tastes. It is literally like reliving the event, and it can completely block out what is happening in the here and now.

Flashbacks can be terrifying both for the person having them, and for anyone who is wishing to support them.

When someone first starts to talk about a traumatic event, they can often experience more flashbacks. What is really frightening is the feeling of losing control over the body's normal responses.

'I didn't have any flashbacks until I started talking to my counsellor. Then they started happening all the time. The trouble was although I was talking to the Counsellor about being attacked, the flashbacks were about what had happened to me when I was little. I thought I was going crazy.

'What helped was trying to see the flashbacks as my mind's way of spring-cleaning itself. All this rubbish needed to come out really. I used to write it all down and then later show it to my Counsellor. It hurt so much, but it was almost like a way of letting the pain out.' Amber

Don't try to fight the flashback; it will continue to force itself. If you can, just let it wash over you.

➢ Give yourself time to recover and take stock of your situation

➢ Think about what will soothe you afterwards

➢ A hot drink

➢ Talking to someone

➢ Sitting in the garden or a brisk walk

➢ Is it something active or calming?

➢ Do take the time to recover. If you rush into the next activity you can become stressed

➢ Take time for you. You deserve it

We discuss flashbacks in more detail on page 213.

Nightmares

Nightmares are another way that survivors may be forced to relive traumatic experiences. They often have the qualities of an intense flashback, and may result in someone shouting out in their sleep, waking disoriented and sweating.

Some people have nightmares every night, and dread going to sleep. They may avoid going to bed altogether, and sleep on chairs or sofas to avoid the trigger of being in a bed. Health can suffer as a result of lack of good quality, restful sleep.

'I used to wake up drenched in sweat, fighting the covers. I thought someone was on top of me, and it'd take ages for me to calm down. I felt too embarrassed to spend the night with someone. They'd have wondered what was going on! I had to be able to switch the light on straight away so I could actually see that I was alone. It took a long time for the nightmares to go away. I still get them sometimes, but nowhere near as much now.'
Raoul

Develop a soothing bedtime routine – hot baths and warm drinks

- ➢ Reduce stimulants like tea and coffee

- ➢ Reduce alcohol – it stops you from sinking into deep, restful sleep, and instead keeps you at the level where nightmares are more likely to happen

- ➢ Make sure you can put the light on immediately when you wake up because it may make you feel safer

- ➢ Keep a drink by the side of the bed

If you feel very distressed after a nightmare:

- ➢ Read or watch something light hearted

- ➢ Only go back to bed when you feel calmer

Anxiety

Many survivors experience constant and lasting states of anxiety that can be experienced as a feeling of being stressed and shaky. They may worry about everything, and feel powerless to help themselves or those they love. They may feel that they have failed at 'everything'; whether relationships, parenting, work or running their home, and worry constantly. They may feel overwhelmed by worrying, as though their minds are on a treadmill with no chance of stepping off.

'I used to lie there every night with all these thoughts going round and round in my head – the kids misbehaving, how I was going to pay this bill or that bill, what the neighbours thought about me, how I was going to get the money to pay for the school trips, the kids needing new trainers. It just went on and on until I couldn't sleep. I felt tired out, and then I just snapped all day at the kids, and then that just got added to the list of all the other things I was worrying about.' Amber

Make yourself a 'worry box'. Write down all the things you are worrying about on separate pieces of paper and put them into your worry box? Instead of worrying constantly, decide that you will focus your worrying time to ten minutes a day. Set aside that time each day when you will concentrate on any worries from the worry box. At the end of that time, decide to leave worrying until the next day.

Acknowledge that some worries are practical, like paying the bills, and some are more to do with your own attitude and beliefs, like feeling you did something wrong. Worrying about problems does not actually solve them, but it can give you a feeling that you are doing something towards finding a solution. However, excessive worrying prevents you from enjoying anything else in your life.

Treat Box

A friend of ours had the idea of having a 'treat box' as well as a worry box. In her treat box she put little things like a new lipstick, a nice soap or a book she wanted to read.

When she feels down, and sometimes when she just feels like she wants a treat, she takes one item from her treat box. She even wraps up the treats so they are surprises.

This is not as ridiculous as it sounds. If you are feeling very down on yourself you need some positive encouragement. The treat box can provide comfort in times of distress.

The suggestion is that the treat box is kept close at hand in your room. When things are bad and there may be temptation to do something you might regret like self-injure, then the treat box may be very useful.

Possible consequences of rape and sexual abuse

Here are some suggestions for your treat box and explanations of how the items can be used to encourage positive thinking:

1. A room fragrance spray

The idea here is that if you feel negative you have to literally spray the room with a lovely positive fragrance. You cannot be feeling down if you have to spray a beautiful sent across the room. You are encouraged to say the fragrance will influence how I feel about my day.

2. Pot pourri

The idea here is to fragrance the room with positive thoughts all the time. The treat box will smell wonderful, and this should encourage you to want to feel good about yourself.

3. Sweets or chocolates

You can give these to yourself as a treat to cheer you up and also as an encouragement and reward for positive thinking.

4. A mascot

In the box should be a figure or teddy. This figure can act as your guardian or mascot. They will be given the gift of knowledge. If you imagine that they know all about you, then they will know how to remind you of the positive things you have achieved during the day. Psychologically the treat box will helps provide simple guidance to positive self-determination.

The figure can hold some positive words in their hands that you can take out and use to help focus you for the day. The act of taking positive words out of a box and displaying them will encourage you to take charge of how you would like to feel. It can be difficult at times to resist giving in to despair, so we need to constantly reinforce the positive.

Here are some of the simple sentences you might have on some flashcards for your figure to show you each day:

- 'I can be a success'

- 'I deserve to have a good day'

- 'I am enthusiastic today'

- 'I am amazing'

- 'I am actively engaged in my own destiny'

- 'I do feel good about myself'

- 'I am feeling good'

- 'I will be positive today'

5. A photo album

A suggestion is that you might like to have a photo album. There you can put all the pictures that mean something to you. In a moment of sadness you can look at the pictures to encourage you. What is good about your life now? You do have some good memories. You do have some people around who care. By having the album you can add photographs and cards and any thing else that you want to store there.

6. Candles

Candles are a special treat to put in your box. If you light them in a room they can give a special ambiance. There are many that are scented. They can be a reward to calm you. (Do remember to blow them out afterwards.)

7. Bath treats

Bath bombs and special bath oils can be put in the treat box for special pampering. Do treat yourself to a relaxing bath. This helps calm you down.

8. Massage oils

Massage has great power to relax and soothe. You can use aromatherapy oils to massage your own hands and feet. If you have not experienced much positive touch in your life, then massaging yourself can allow you to experience how it feels for your body to be touched in a sensual way that is safe and all can benefit from that treat.

8. Incense sticks

Incense sticks are fun to also fragrance the room for a positive reward.

9. Flowers

By the side of the treat box there should be some fresh flowers. These can help lift the mood. You are encouraged to wait to see what flower will open next. If you are depressed this simple technique of giving yourself something to look forward to may help.

 *It is important that you personalise the treat box. What will you put into your treat box? It may help to make this list even if you do not physically make a box.*

_____

_____

_____

_____

_____

_____

_____

PHYSICAL HEALTH

Sexual assaults can result directly in physical injuries – trauma to the genitals and internal injuries. There may be bladder and bowel weaknesses caused by such injuries. Back injuries are quite common. Sexually transmitted infections may also be passed on, and sometimes scabies or body lice can also be transmitted.

In some cases, rape may result in pregnancy. One of the less well-known effects of shock is that a woman's body may immediately release an ovum (egg) so that chances of pregnancy are increased.

> ➢ A physical check-up as soon after a sexual assault as can be coped with, including a pregnancy test if appropriate

> ➢ Rape and Sexual Abuse Support Services will often accompany someone to a hospital or GP surgery if medical attention or tests are needed

> ➢ The morning-after pill can actually be taken up to 72 hours after intercourse, and can be obtained at chemists. Some chemists may not dispense the morning-after pill because of their beliefs or faith. You may want to check this before going to shop

Possible consequences of rape and sexual abuse

If your faith or own beliefs prevent you from using the morning-after pill and you become pregnant, then do seek support and counselling to help you cope and bond with your baby, or to discuss what options may be available to you for ongoing support.

If there are worries about sexually transmitted infections, including HIV, then Genito-Urinary Clinics (GUM Clinics) will often offer a fast-track service. These are completely confidential and will not release information, even to a GP without your permission.

If you are experiencing ongoing problems, like bowel or bladder weakness or back problems, where intimate examinations may be necessary, then it may help to talk to your doctor about the trauma. It will give them the opportunity to be more sensitive to your needs during examinations.

Some of the most surprising research findings have been those that identify where someone's general physical health is affected by the constant stress of trauma. Links have been identified with many conditions:

- ➢ Increased rates of heart disease and cancer
- ➢ Chronic lung conditions
- ➢ Arthritis
- ➢ Chronic physical pain
- ➢ Irritable bowel syndrome
- ➢ Epilepsy
- ➢ Eating disorders

Stress has the damaging effect of lowering the body's immune system and making it more vulnerable to health problems.

Some survivors experience something called somatisation. This is where emotional distress is turned into physical symptoms that have no other apparent cause – headaches, back pain, stomach pains.

In addition to all the above, we have found that survivors do not generally take good care of their own health, as part of a general pattern of undervaluing themselves. Neglect in childhood may also mean that normal patterns of eating and sleeping have never been established, and are difficult to take on board in adult life.

➢ Seek out specialist support services and helplines to target specific concerns. There is a list of agencies on page 323

➢ Treat yourself as you would a child – you need good food, plenty of sleep and sufficient exercise for your body and mind to work at its best

➢ Research has shown that writing about your feelings for twenty minutes a day is useful in helping to manage arthritis and chronic pain

MENTAL　　　　　　　　　　　　　　**HEALTH**

Research findings　　　　　　　　　　have　revealed

that over half of all female psychiatric inpatients report childhood sexual abuse. The links between sexual violence and mental ill health are now becoming very well recognised.

There are also links with mental ill health that many workers within the voluntary sector support groups would acknowledge, including as a factor in developing schizophrenia. Unfortunately, research is still needed to substantiate these links.

At the moment, we feel the following is important for survivors to know.

Depression

Depression is a common response to trauma experienced by both women and men. Symptoms include disturbed sleeping patterns like finding it difficult to get to sleep and then waking up early. Some people sleep far more than usual. Energy levels are very low, and it can feel like limbs are weighted down with lead. People lose interest in themselves and have poor self-care, even neglecting to wash properly. They may lose their appetite or comfort eat, so their diets become unbalanced.

There is often little interest in what is happening around them, and concentration can be poor.

Depression is something that can creep up slowly on someone, so that they become used to feeling low and not caring about what is happening to them.

Post Traumatic Stress/Rape Trauma/Complex Post Traumatic Stress

The symptoms of Post Traumatic Stress include:

➢ Nightmares and/or flashbacks
➢ Feeling depressed
➢ Constantly being on edge and jumpy

> ➢ Irritability and mood swings

When someone goes through a traumatic event, it is normal to experience all or a combination of the above responses for some time afterwards. Post Traumatic Stress is diagnosed when these responses persist for longer than three months.

However, we would encourage anyone who experiences such responses for more than six weeks to seek support through their GP. It is becoming more widely recognised that earlier support for Post Traumatic Stress can be very helpful.

Post Traumatic Stress symptoms are linked to one-off events where someone experiences a life threatening or life changing situation, including rape. Some people refer to Rape Trauma Syndrome rather than Post Traumatic Stress.

Symptoms of Rape Trauma Syndrome

People suffering from Rape Trauma often wish to avoid thinking and talking about what has happened. In the immediate days following the rape, they may seek out support initially but then decide that it is less painful for them to carry on talking about what has happened. In the short term, this is probably true. However, avoiding talking about the rape will not make the effects go away or not happen. People may experience fear of going out (agoraphobia), suffer from depression, have problems with intimate relationships, suffer from self-blame and have persistent flashbacks or nightmares.

What we would say is that although it will be painful to continue talking about the rape, this will ease and the long term effects will be more easily coped with. Over time, people who have persisted with support report better levels of coping and general emotional wellbeing than those who do not continue with support.

There is now a growing awareness that although Post Traumatic Stress or Rape Trauma is useful in describing the responses and effects of a single traumatic event, people who have experienced longer term,

Possible consequences of rape and sexual abuse

chronic trauma have a deeper level of psychological hurt. Long-term traumatic events, like childhood sexual abuse, physical abuse or domestic violence, can cause such deep psychological wounds that a person's sense of self and ability to cope with everyday life is damaged.

Dr. Judith Herman, a psychiatrist based at Harvard University, has developed a new diagnosis of Complex Post Traumatic Stress which describes the psychological impact of long term trauma. The kinds of experiences that can lead to Complex Post Traumatic Stress are situations where someone has been abused, either physically, emotionally or sexually, over a long period of time (months or even years) where they have been unable to escape:

> - Child sexual abuse
> - Organised child sexual abuse
> - Long-term domestic violence
> - Long-term physical abuse
> - Prostitution brothels
> - Prisoner of war camps

The symptoms of Complex Post Traumatic Stress include:

> - Depression and suicidal thoughts
> - Outbursts of anger
> - Feeling detached from thoughts and physical sensations
> - Reliving memories
> - Feeling helpless
> - Feeling ashamed or guilty
> - Feeling different from other people
> - Believing the perpetrator to be 'all-powerful'
> - Being obsessed by thoughts of revenge
> - Being or feeling isolated from others
> - Mistrusting others but also constantly looking for a rescuer
> - Loss of faith and belief

Not surprisingly, these symptoms often lead a survivor to avoid thinking or talking about their experiences. They may choose drugs or alcohol as a way of numbing or altering their feelings and thoughts or as a way of blanking out flashbacks and nightmares. Many survivors also self-injure in some way.

In the past there has been a mistaken belief that when someone has been repeatedly victimised this means they are a weak person. Survivors have often felt that they have been 'blamed by the system' for being victims rather than helped and supported appropriately. It has also meant that effective treatments have not been offered because survivors have been mistakenly diagnosed with personality disorders, like Borderline, Dependent or Masochistic Personality Disorder. Our prisons and hospital wards may be full of people who are actually suffering from Complex Post Traumatic Stress that remains undiagnosed and unrecognised. Some of the symptoms may even have contributed to anti-social or criminal behaviour.

We hope that the new diagnosis of Complex Post Traumatic Stress will help to ensure that survivors are no longer 'blamed' for the symptoms their traumatic experiences have caused, and that society and 'the system' can start to respond with the care and understanding survivors deserve.

If you feel you are suffering from Complex Post Traumatic Stress, then you must remember that this is a new diagnosis proposed by Dr. Judith Lewis Herman, MD and that your GP or other health worker may not be familiar with her work. Ask them to find out more (there is plenty of information on the internet, and Dr. Herman has written about her work: Trauma and Recovery - The Aftermath of Violence from Domestic Violence to Political Terror).

In the next Chapter, Coping With Stress, we look at different ways of coping with traumatic stress.

Dissociation

In general life, all our senses are joined up and interconnected. Our emotions, physical sensations, thinking and behaviour are all linked together to build up our responses to ourselves, other people and the world.

Dissociation is where one or more aspects of these senses are disjointed from the others. This means that reactions to what is happening, either internally or in the outside world, are not co-ordinated and do not correlate to what is actually happening. People may respond without realising why they are reacting in that way; they may feel emotionally numb, like the world around them is not real; they may experience physical numbness, not registering pain or discomfort; and they may lose contact with their surroundings.

There are five different types of dissociation that can be experienced either on their own or in any combination:

1.   Amnesia - when someone cannot remember an event or experience, or when important personal information is forgotten
2.   Depersonalisation – feeling that your body is not real or is changing in some way. This can include out-of-body sensations, when it feels like you are watching yourself in a movie Derealisation – when the world and people around you seem unreal. You might see objects changing colour or shape, or may think that people are robots
3.   Identity confusion – not knowing who you are as a person and feeling unable to define yourself
4.   Identity alteration – a change in your behaviour that other people would notice

Dissociation happens quite often in everyday life – when daydreaming, for example, or putting something down and then forgetting where it is – but if someone dissociates constantly then their day-to-day life can be disrupted. However, many people who suffer from dissociative disorders hold down responsible jobs and successfully raise families. They often feel ashamed of the symptoms they experience Dissociative Identity Disorder (DID), formerly known as multiple personalities, is linked with extreme or ritual childhood abuse. This is a condition where someone experiences one or more different identity states. There may be gaps in time ranging from a few minutes to weeks or months. Each identity state may be aware or unaware of the others, and may exhibit completely different behaviours. Self-injuring behaviour is common, and the other identity states may be unaware of the identity that has the harming behaviour, and unable to do anything to prevent it happening.

There is generally low recognition of dissociative distress or DID and diagnosis and treatment may be something that someone has to actively seek out. Some medical practitioners do not acknowledge DID as a condition. However, dissociation can be assessed using questionnaires designed for this, but it is essential that they are administered by a trained health professional. There have been cases where someone has been receiving care through mental health services for many years with little improvement in their symptoms, but who responds extremely well when dissociative distress is recognized and appropriate treatment offered.

Symptoms that people with dissociative conditions may have include:

➢ Depression
➢ Mood swings
➢ Anxiety attacks
➢ Panic attacks
➢ Suicidal thoughts
➢ Self-injury
➢ Headaches
➢ Hearing voices
➢ Sleep disorders
➢ Phobias

Possible consequences of rape and sexual abuse

> Alcohol and drug abuse
> Eating disorders
> Obsessive compulsive behaviour

These symptoms may be connected to the dissociative condition or may mean that someone is also suffering from a separate condition.

When someone has DID, the above symptoms may only be present when a particular identity has the control of the person's behaviour, thoughts and feelings, and not present at other times.

Effects of dissociation

Many people who experience dissociation feel embarrassed and ashamed of the effects. They often use coping strategies to help them manage the dissociation, like notebooks and reminders, and attempt to hide their problems and difficulties from those around them. Many sufferers are able to have responsible jobs and raise families. Some TV programmes have portrayed people with dissociative disorders as very obviously and quickly 'switching' from identity to identity. This is misleading since very few people experience dissociation in this way. Often, someone with a dissociative condition will have difficulty in recognising what is happening to them. The following effects might be noticed:

> Gaps in time that can be from a few minutes up to years
> Suddenly finding yourself somewhere with no recollection of how you got there
> Forgetting important appointments and meetings
> Using different styles of handwriting
> Forgetting a learned skill
> Finding that you have a learned skill that you do not remember studying
> Feeling that you don't recognise a familiar place
> Feeling unreal or detached from reality
> Feeling detached from your emotions

- ➤ Loss of sensation in parts of your body
- ➤ Not recognising yourself in the mirror
- ➤ Internal voices and conversations within yourself
- ➤ Behaving differently
- ➤ Other people commenting that you have behaved differently
- ➤ Feeling like there are other personalities inside you, including child-like personalities
- ➤ Feeling confused about your sexuality or gender

If you are experiencing symptoms that lead you to believe you may be suffering from a dissociative condition or DID, then you can find support and information at:

www.firstperson.plural.org.uk

Schizophrenia

This does not mean someone has two personalities, or has a split mind. Schizophrenia is diagnosed when a range of symptoms are present. These include hearing voices or having visual hallucinations. People may also develop delusions and paranoia, where they feel that they are being got at, or put down by others. Sometimes people believe that they are being communicated with through the TV or radio.

Symptoms often start to occur in men in their late teenage years and in women a few years later. Some survivors may experience flashbacks where they re-experience hearing an abuser talking to them. In some cases, this has lead to misdiagnosis of schizophrenia.

If someone is experiencing many symptoms of mental distress, then it is vital that they seek medical care as soon as possible

➤ Although many people resist taking tablets, in some cases, medication may be needed to help with symptoms

➤ Support groups and helplines offer direct support, and some are open 24 hours a day

➤ Psychiatric and psychological services provide a support network within the community

➤ Community Psychiatric Nurses will support someone at home and provide links to other support services

➤ Specialist support services for survivors of rape and sexual abuse will provide counselling and support directly linked to trauma responses

SELF-BELIEF - LIFE SITUATIONS

Experiencing trauma in general has a damaging effect on someone's sense of self-worth and often then an impact on how their lives progress. Survivors often experience a wide range of problems resulting from a lack of belief in their own value and worth.

Loss of trust

We believe that the single most damaging effect of sexual violation is the complete loss of trust that follows. People are not safe. The world is not safe. And even more, fear of being judged or seen as dirty or shameful, can prevent people finding the support they need.

Low self-worth

Many survivors will agree that they suffer from lack of confidence and low self-esteem. Self-doubt is common, even as far as doubting what has happened. Survivors may suffer from low expectations from life, believing that they aren't 'good enough' to achieve. There may even be financial problems, when survivors find it difficult to focus on practical matters, or fail to plan properly. Planning and looking ahead seem to be difficult tasks for many survivors.

Here are some of the feelings that you may recognise. In this exercise you might wish to identify how you have felt at some point and what you want to be different

I am different to other people

_____

_____

_____

_____

Possible consequences of rape and sexual abuse

Why I am the same as other people

_____

_____

_____

I have thought about suicide

_____

_____

_____

Why I want to be alive

_____

_____

_____

I have lied to others about my life

_____

_____

_____

Why I do not need to lie about what has happened to me

_____

_____

_____

I am harsh on myself

_____

_____

_____

Why I should be kind to myself

_____

_____

_____

I do not trust myself

_____

_____

_____

Why I can trust myself

_____

_____

_____

Go out and join a gym. There are others there to try to get fit. You will meet people. There are lots of activities and exercise routines there. Some people like all the jumping around. Certainly there may be lots of laughter and this will produce lots of the right feelings in the body. Keep fit classes or aerobics are not to everyone's taste, but it is a good idea to get healthy

Possible consequences of rape and sexual abuse

Mood swings

Relationships may have suffered due to mood swings and feelings of insecurity. Emotions veering from sadness to rage, or happiness to despair, mean that survivors can be very difficult to be in a relationship with.

See the section on Mood Swings at page 52.

Parenting problems

As parents, many survivors find it difficult to discipline children and are too lenient. They struggle to identify what the appropriate boundaries are for parents. Some survivors are so afraid that their child might have a similar abusive experience to themselves, that they become extremely strict and are unable to allow their child the appropriate freedom to grow and develop.

If you haven't experienced appropriate parenting, how do you become a good parent yourself?

Remaining childless

Sadly, for some survivors, the thought that their own child might go through the same experience as they have means that they make the decision to never bring a child into the world who might suffer as they have, and they remain childless through choice.

They may fear that any partner they have could be a potential abuser, and decide they never want any child of theirs to experience what they have experienced. Some survivors feel that the world is not a safe or good place to bring children into.

NURTURE

We all need to nurture ourselves and others. There is the whole debate about nature and nurture. If we can, we must see the positive need to develop the right lifestyle for children, to nurture them in a loving environment. With encouragement even people who start out with major disadvantages can make progress.

'I didn't understand what nurturing myself meant. It didn't seem relevant to me. I just thought I had to get on with my life as best I could and put up with how I was feeling. Eventually, though, I knew I had to do something to help myself feel better. It's strange, though, because as I started to think more about what I wanted the more I started to like myself. It's okay for me to have things and to feel good. I deserve little luxuries just as much as anyone else.' Niles

---

Feeling unloved or unable to show love to others

Feelings of low self-worth may lead survivors to doubt that they can be loved by anyone. Many survivors feel that they have to try and please everyone else, or they will not be liked or accepted. When you do not value yourself, it can be impossible to believe that someone else thinks you are worthwhile, let alone someone to love.

Possible consequences of rape and sexual abuse

This can lead to a paradoxical response to loved ones – if we believe ourselves to be worthless, then someone who loves us must be either deluded or mistaken. Because we doubt their true feelings, then we punish them by being cold towards them, or getting angry. In the face of this, the more someone shows us love, the more difficult it is to believe them and so we push away the very people who want to share love with us.

How you have been nurturing yourself recently?

_____

_____

_____

_____

_____

_____

_____

_____

_____

_____

_____

_____

_____

_____

_____

Sexual abstinence

Sexual intimacy is understandably a difficult area for many survivors. Both men and women may decide that they do not wish to have a sexual relationship. It might be that a person feels upset about the past, and they choose not to have a sexual relationship with anyone. This is because they might feel dirty or unlovable or they are afraid they might be hurt again. Some people may experience flashbacks when they are touched in a certain way and this can prevent them from experiencing any pleasure in a sexual way. They choose to remain single or in a relationship without sexual contact.

Promiscuity

On the other hand, when someone has been sexually abused, they may confuse sex with love and have many different sexual partners seeking love. However, in their understanding, sex has no real emotional meaning and therefore no matter how many times they have sex or how many partners they have, there is never a sense of satisfaction or fulfilment. Low self-esteem may also drive people to seek out lots of different sexual partners as a way of trying to prove they are desirable. This often backfires, as ultimately what they really want is love and not sexual activity.

Prostitution

Many survivors will acknowledge that their attitudes towards sex and sexuality have been affected by their abusive experiences. For some people, there are no boundaries around sexual experiences, and their sense of self-worth is so low they see prostitution as nothing more than another activity. Their bodies have already been violated without their consent or choice, and there may even be a sense of using their bodies themselves for their own gain, or to discover a sense of power over others – particularly sexual power.

Many women and men who use prostitution to fund drug habits have been sexually abused as children.

Possible consequences of rape and sexual abuse

Some young people leave home because of abusive situations. They may then find themselves homeless and living on the streets with no opportunity to support themselves financially. They are extremely vulnerable to being drawn into prostitution as a way of gaining money, and may be approached by people looking specifically for young girls or boys.

Survivors of sexual abuse and violence can find it difficult to see themselves as wholesome and deserving of respect. They have not been shown respect by others, and have therefore not been able to develop their own sense of self-respect. Their behaviour may be highly risky, putting themselves in danger of physical violence and sexual assaults, and may involve other risky behaviour, like misusing substances.

If someone has made a choice to become a sex worker, rather than through necessity to fund a drug habit, then that is their own personal decision. If someone feels that they have no other opportunities or places no value on themselves and drift into prostitution, then that choice will be damaging to their personalities and lives. Specialist health workers can support someone who wishes to escape from sex work.

Confusion about sexual identity

Many male survivors, and a significant number of female survivors, develop a confused view of their own sexuality. Men may ask themselves if they have been sexually abused or raped by men because they 'gave out the wrong signals'. This means they are questioning their sexual identity, and possibly blaming themselves, if they feel they have too feminine traits. Or they may feel that being sexually abused has made them prefer male sexual partners.

Some women feel that because of their experiences of sexual abuse as a child, they are unable to have a fulfilling relationship with a man and believe that being sexually abused has 'turned' them lesbian or bisexual.

You need to know that rape and sexual abuse do not happen because of anything the victim does or says. Abuse happens because an abuser takes a selfish decision to abuse someone who is more vulnerable and who cannot defend or protect themselves. It may be that boys who have more feminine characteristics are targeted by abusers because they already feel different or vulnerable.

In the confusion that many gay or bisexual people feel as they first discover their own sexuality, they may blame abusive experiences for making them 'different'. There are conflicting theories about the development of sexual identity, but there is a growing understanding that sexual identity is determined while a baby is still in the womb. Negative sexual experiences will affect how somehow sees themselves, but they do not have the ultimate power to determine whether someone is heterosexual, gay or bisexual.

Suicidal thoughts

In our experience, every survivor we have come into contact with has considered suicide, and often made at least one attempt at suicide, at some point.

With the world seeming to be such an uncaring, untrustworthy place, and when they place so little value on themselves, there is no surprise that a survivor might feel that their life is not worth continuing. Constant and ongoing emotional pain and an inability to believe that things can improve, mean that survivors are particularly vulnerable to suicidal thoughts. Research has shown that survivors are up to eleven times more likely to attempt suicide.

> ➤ Build up a support network of friends, partners, carers, specialist services, helplines, and health workers

> ➤ Specialist support services for survivors offer counselling, advice and support specific to survivors' needs

> ➤ Develop positive coping strategies for the tough times, including using this book for ideas

> # INSPIRATION
>
> All kinds of different things can inspire us – sometimes the world around us can inspire good feelings. Sometimes another person who has coped with adversity or who has achieved something we admire can inspire us by their example.

Crime and antisocial behaviour

There is a direct impact on our communities and our society, as a result of the psychological reactions in some individuals caused by the abuse of children and rape of adults. Alcohol is often a factor in domestic violence situations, and both male and female survivors will report that they have been aggressive towards their partners. There are links between crime and drug and alcohol misuse. These behaviours are often implicated in crimes committed by people funding drug habits, or aggression linked to intoxication.

The majority of individuals convicted of sex offences are male, but the vast majority of victims of childhood sexual abuse do not go on to become abusers. One study of sex offenders who were claiming to have been sexually abused themselves, showed that after they were told they would be subject to a lie detector test, the numbers dropped from 67% to 29%.

Abusing others

Sadly, we have to acknowledge that a number of people who have been abused will themselves go on to abuse others. Both men and women who have been sexually abused may later sexually abuse children themselves. Research is suggesting that this abusive behaviour will often start in adolescence. When someone does go on to abuse others, they have usually experienced more severe and extreme forms of abuse themselves.

Sometimes, women who have been sexually abused do not protect their own children from abuse by their partners. They may be fully aware that their children are being abused, but decide to ignore this out of misplaced loyalty for their partners, or because they fear the consequences of confronting their partners.

Since their own boundaries were violated, they seem unable to maintain appropriate boundaries for their own children and their own relationships. However, there is a very damaging myth that suggests that if a man has been sexually abused, then it is inevitable that he will also become an abuser. This myth has devastating effects on men seeking support when they have been sexually abused themselves, since they have not wanted to be thought of as potential abusers.

Current research has shown that out of eight male survivors, one will become an abuser themselves. And, we must remind ourselves of the following:

> ➤ Most survivors do not report their experiences
> ➤ Statistics for perpetrators are based on self-reporting by perpetrators, which has proved to be very unreliable, with significant numbers of perpetrators falsely claiming to have been abused themselves in mitigation of their own actions

Our experience in working with male survivors is that their response towards sexual abuse of children is of absolute horror and disgust. They feel appalled that anyone might think they themselves would be capable of hurting a child in any way, and are often oversensitive to situations where children may be vulnerable or at risk of abuse. They may feel they have to be extra cautious around how they react and respond to children – how they hug them or kiss them, or whether they are alone with a child. This can make parenting and family relationships strained and unhappy.

Reactive abuse

Children who have been sexually abused may also act out sexual behaviour on their peers.

Possible consequences of rape and sexual abuse

There was a nine-year-old boy who was being abused by his cousin, who was fifteen years old. The cousin abused the boy by engaging in inappropriate behaviour. This started when he came to baby sit and he suggested they have a bath together. It was here that the cousin performed oral sex on the boy. In subsequent visits he encouraged the boy to do it back to him. So the young boy became interested in bodies and discussions about sex. He then persuaded his friend, who was the same age, to join him in sexual play. As he grew up he was deeply regretful. He suffered deep remorse over his actions. He knew that he had done wrong and wished he could have undone his behaviour.

This is known as reactive abuse. A child's behaviour has become sexualised and they act this out with other children. They have had their own personal boundaries violated, and at the time cannot appreciate why it is wrong to behave sexually towards other children. Later in life they may experience very great feelings of remorse and self-loathing.

Some young people engage in sexual games with their friends as they are growing up. This is normal child-like curiosity about sex and should not be regarded as abusive unless force or coercion has been used. What we want to say is that the experience of childhood sexual abuse is never an excuse for someone sexually abusing another person. In fact, the vast majority of survivors become determined never to allow their own children to endure the same experiences.

We do believe that it is vital that adolescent abusers receive appropriate treatment and intervention programmes before their abusive behaviour can become ingrained and become a part of their adult lives. There is now growing recognition of the need for appropriate treatment programmes.

If you have any concerns about your own or someone else's behaviour towards a child, then the Stop It Now! UK and Ireland campaign offers a helpline that anyone can call. They will offer advice and referral to services for further support.

NEGATIVE COPING STRATEGIES

All the negative impacts on emotional, psychological and physical health listed above really bring home how difficult survivors can find it just coping with their lives. They are on almost constant overload emotionally and psychologically, and often physical symptoms and conditions add to their low sense of self-worth and poor relationships with others.

You shouldn't be surprised, then, if negative coping strategies develop. However, we stress again that not everyone who has been raped or abused will do any or all of these things. Some coping strategies offer short-term relief, but at the expense of health and relationships, and in some cases (substance addictions, for instance) at the expense of freedom.

UNCONDITIONAL SELF-ACCEPTANCE

This means that you can accept yourself for who you are and how that makes you behave. We all of us sometimes cannot come up to the high ideals that we have set ourselves. If we beat ourselves up over our failures we might just feel worse and stop ourselves from celebrating our real successes.

'It has taken years for me to accept who I am. Nothing ever seemed to have been how I would have chosen it to be, including me. Now I feel proud of the way I have coped and how I have got on in my life. I know I have done my best, and no-one can do any more than that.' Niles

---

How do you feel about your own sense of self-acceptance?

_____

_____

_____

_____

_____

_____

_____

_____

_____

_____

_____

_____

_____

_____

_____

_____

_____

_____

Alcohol and drug misuse

Research is now showing that some survivors use substances to manage their trauma responses – the flashbacks, nightmares, anxiety, panic attacks, lack of confidence and feelings of low self-worth. There is a growing recognition that this has to be taken into account when working with someone with substance addiction. Are they using drugs to gain control over their symptoms? What other activities might soothe or deal with that symptom?

Many survivors will use alcohol and or drugs as a way of escaping painful feelings. They may also use alcohol as a way to relax or help them to sleep. Unfortunately, alcohol has a paradoxical effect. This means that although drinking appears to relax someone, what it actually does is act like a depressant. That's why people who are drunk often end up crying at the end of the night – alcohol makes you feel more depressed. Drinking also prevents the body from getting into the deepest levels of sleep that are the most restful and renewing. Instead, only lighter sleep happens where dreams and nightmares are more common.

Whilst someone is using drugs or alcohol to numb their emotions or to alter their moods, they will remain stuck in the same place emotionally. Drugs and alcohol work too well at numbing emotions. Although it is tough, it is only when the difficult and painful emotions are faced full on that they can be dealt with.

> ➢ Community Drug and Alcohol Services will offer practical support and counselling to deal with the addictions and problems associated with substances

> ➢ Specialist support and counselling from a rape and sexual abuse service will be essential in identifying and dealing with the trauma responses underlying the addictions

Self-injury

This can take many forms. People may cut themselves, scratch themselves, pull hair, swallow objects or toxic substances. The reasons why someone self-injures are as varied and different as individual people themselves, and the same person can use self-injury on different occasions in response to different triggers.

It is generally thought that self-injury is more a female response to difficult situations and feelings, but significant numbers of men also self-injure. Sexual abuse and sexual assault are strongly connected to self-injuring, but many other forms of distress are also linked including bullying, the death of a parent or loved one, chronic illness and mental ill health.

People may self-injure at times in response to feeling numb or unreal. They may not experience any pain as they self-injure, but may feel a sense of relief or release. Sometimes someone may feel overwhelmed with difficult and painful emotions that they cannot find another way to express, and they may use self-injury as a way of turning their emotional pain into a physical pain that can then be soothed. Or they may feel intense self-hatred and disgust and wish to punish themselves in a physical way.

In the same way that drugs and alcohol can offer some short-term relief, self-injuring also offers a kind of relief from painful emotions.

Unfortunately, the sense of relief someone can feel is often very short-lived, and they often feel even worse about themselves because they have self-injured again. This can lead to a repeating cycle of self-injury that becomes addictive in itself. It may be that when someone experiences higher levels of stress, then they self-injure more often or more seriously. They may even find that after stopping self-injuring, they can return to this way of coping in response to new stresses.

Attitudes to people who self-injure are slowly changing, but many survivors still find that medical workers do not treat them appropriately. There have been instances where someone has had stitches put in without any anaesthetic being offered. Hopefully, this kind of response is a thing of the past, but health professionals can still feel frustrated and puzzled that someone has harmed themselves, and often work without sufficient training or supervision to enable them to offer the most appropriate support.

We believe that self-injury is part of the range of normal human responses to intense emotional distress as a result of trauma, where someone focuses their distress on themselves rather than on someone else. In our understanding, it is a more socially responsible way of coping than taking it out on others. But, we also believe that survivors deserve to live free from further pain and suffering and want to encourage everyone who uses self-injury to seek out new, different and creative ways of expressing and experiencing their emotions.

There are specialist support groups for people who self-injure, and these can offer vital support and insight for people who have become dependent on self-injuring as a way of coping with their situation. A list of groups is provided on page 323. Many counsellors and supporters also struggle to fully understand what is motivating someone to injure themselves. They may refuse to work with someone who is still using self-injury as a way of coping. This is not generally a helpful attitude. What tends to be more supportive and helpful is when alternatives to self-injuring can be discussed and linked up to the feelings that self-injury is being used to cope with.

Workoholism

Throwing yourself into work can be a really effective way to avoid acknowledging painful emotions, and like other coping behaviours it is also addictive because it offers some relief and respite from thinking about past experiences or difficult current situations.

We're not just talking about paid work here either. Any kind of work activity, whether in the home, in paid work or in a voluntary capacity, can be used as a substitute for acknowledging feelings. Working to perfection may allow you to feel you have achieved something – higher productivity at work, or a spotless house – and this may temporarily boost your sense of self-worth. It may even seem that you are coping really well because you are refusing to acknowledge painful emotions.

But when it becomes impossible to refuse to complete a task or refuse a request to do something, then self-esteem can start to plummet. Overwork and exhaustion can lead to feelings of being inadequate and worthless.

The painful emotions do not simply disappear either. They are still there, festering underneath all the frantic activity, and ready to burst out when you feel low or when you become too tired to continue with the overwork.

Like any other coping strategy, whilst you might be working obsessively and not allowing yourself to appreciate your feelings and circumstances, then you never allow yourself the time and space to deal with the painful emotions and realisations of what has happened to you. Your family and personal lives also suffer because all your time is taken up working, and you may even be too exhausted to devote energy to personal relationships.

In this case, actually acknowledging that there is a problem is a major step forward for someone in being able to choose to deal with the pain and move on to a more rounded and fulfilling life.

Possible consequences of rape and sexual abuse

> If you are a survivor yourself, then listen to what your friends and loved ones tell you. It may be that it is a partner, parent or friend who first notices that someone is working obsessively and not allowing themselves personal time for leisure and relaxation

> Specialist support and counselling may be needed to support someone in dealing with painful past experiences and emotions

In certain circumstances it can be that a daily survival routine needs to be established. No one is under any delusion how far away from feeling successful someone may be. Yet success can come from being honest with your family. Coping is a form of success.

'I have been successful in taking control of my life and living it the way I want it to be.' Raoul

> I am successful because I can see where I have lost out but have also won

> I have things in my life that I can hold on to. I can accept disappointment

> I can be successful when I do this small task well and with a free conscience

SUCCESSFUL

Sometimes it can be impossible to imagine how you could feel successful. Some people may feel very down. Their family situation may be in a crisis.

They may feel a failure in personal relationships. They may feel a failure as a parent. They may not be coping with their children's behaviour.

Some survivors are still suffering with rage years after the abuse. They may seek some form of revenge. They may see a lack of justice in society against those who have harmed them. Some are just coping the best way they can. Some have survived the ups and downs of being a parent. Some have endured disappointment with their children. Some have even seen their own children become victims of abuse.

This can lead survivors to the very edge of their being.

The last thing they can feel is successful.

Some survivors are seeking love from people who are not suitable and these people are manipulating their relationships. They cannot bear the thought of being rejected and cling to hope that someone will love them.

Yet even in the darkest times, small progress is possible.

It might be necessary to sit down and take stock of where you have come from and where you need to get to. This can happen as a family or as an individual. This can happen in small steps.

Success can happen in small particulars.

Here are some thoughts you might like to explore. What are your thoughts on these comments?

'I am successful in nurturing myself.' Niles

_____

_____

_____

'I am successful in managing my feelings.' Raoul

_____

_____

_____

'I am successful in respecting my own body.' Raoul

_____

_____

_____

'I am successful in living another day.' Amber

_____

_____

_____

'I am successful in finding new ways of expressing my feelings.' Amber

_____

_____

_____

Please give yourself permission to be a success in believing you can do something. It may be a large or small task but you have to believe you can do it.

Use your journal to create a successful page. Draw, stick, write - make it as interesting as possible.

CHAPTER 9

COPING WITH STRESS

It might be that at this point you may be feeling low and not wish to continue reading any further. You might feel shocked after reading about the possible consequences of sexual violence.

You may have recognised how your own life and health have been affected. What you need to know is that how you are feeling is a normal reaction to stress caused by trauma. It might be that you feel overwhelmed at this point, and yet we are encouraging you to take some positive steps to help yourself.

Stress makes many people ill. There is a lot of evidence to show this is the case. So here is some practical advice. At this point you need to get your body armour on.

> ➢ Make sure you won't be disturbed

> ➢ Sit quietly and allow yourself to breathe normally

> ➢ Close your eyes and relax

> ➢ Now imagine that you are putting on glowing transparent armour
> – you can see and hear and feel through the armour, but nothing
> can come through to harm you

> ➢ Imagine you are holding a huge shield – around the edge are
> engraved the words 'Truth', 'Strength' and 'Freedom'. In the
> centre are engraved the words: 'My Spirit Cannot Be Harmed'

If you want to, you can imagine yourself going about your everyday life
wearing your glowing armour. See how you feel when you have your
armour and shield to protect you.

Stress has both physical and emotional effects. The impact of sexual
abuse and violence can make many survivors become accustomed to
living with a constant level of stress. This is unhealthy for both your
mind and your body.

Physical signs of stress:

> ➢ Rapid heartbeat

> ➢ Headaches

> ➢ Stomach aches

> ➢ Muscle tension

Emotional signs of stress:

> ➢ Excitement

> ➢ Exhilaration

> ➢ Joy

Also

> ➢ Frustration

> ➢ Nervousness

> ➢ Discouragement

> ➢ Anxiety

> ➢ Anger

Your life choices might have put you under a constant pressure, as well. In any event, the emotional responses to trauma mean that stress can be continual. Every minute of the day is a fight. Stress has a directly physical impact on the body.

During stressful times blood sugar is raised, fat/cholesterol levels go up and adrenaline levels goes up. What this means is that your body is then vulnerable to a range of illnesses – heart disease, strokes, stomach ulcers, irritable bowel syndrome, diabetes.

If your body feels constantly on red alert then as a result your mind will also be more sensitive. Little things become major incidents. Concentration suffers and you may have outbursts of frustration.

Your body and mind are being disturbed by the body's physical reaction to stress.

Relaxation: There are many CDs and tapes available these days that offer techniques to help relieve stress and we would encourage you to try them out. We've found that the biggest winner with de-stressing is this: if you believe it is doing you good then it probably is. Listening to music has the power to change your mood. Don't choose depressing music! There is a theory that everything can be healed with music. Music can sooth your troubled mind. It is very important to listen to music that can calm you down in difficult times.

Negative Coping Strategies for Managing Stress

Many survivors develop negative ways of coping with stress reactions. Alcohol and drugs can be used to blot out memories in the short-term but the long-term they create problems of their own through dependencies. There can be harm to your mental health and your judgement can be impaired so that close relationships and work are affected.

Some survivors respond to trauma related stress by aggressively defending themselves. Unfortunately, they often behave aggressively towards people who are close to them – the wrong targets – and hurt or drive away loved ones.

Alternatively, some survivors manage stress by isolating themselves from others to protect themselves from being hurt again or to avoid situations where they may feel upset or angry. While this will manage your emotions, it will not allow you to take part in normal social activities, and you will have an increased risk of continuing depression leading to further isolation.

Positive Coping Strategies for Managing Stress

Although the effects of Post Traumatic Stress and Complex Post Traumatic Stress can be very persistent, there are many things that you can do to lessen the impact of stress in your life. Positive coping strategies for managing stress will allow you to develop new lifestyles that encourage healing.

One of the most important ways you can combat stress is to find out about why you are reacting in this way. This book will provide some of this information. Joining a support group also provides direct support from other people who have experienced trauma. Groups give you an opportunity to share tried and tested ways of coping with stress and best ways of managing responses.

Another positive coping strategy you can use for managing stress is to be aware that if you feel you are reaching a crisis point you make sure to seek out counselling or individual support. There is strength in realising when you need extra support to get you through a tough time and this can protect you from becoming more depressed or upset.

CARING

Some survivors feel that their experience of suffering has made them more caring as a person – more sensitive and understanding when other people are having problems. This may come out in the way they show caring for their families and friends. They may be more patient when someone is upset or good listeners when someone is troubled.

But this might also be about caring for yourself. We have advice on how to pamper yourself. Take time for you. Nourish yourself by doing some of those things you would like to do. It is a great quality to care both for others as well as yourself.

'I have finally given myself permission to enjoy relaxing in the bath. This is 'me time' when I can luxuriate in the bubbles and totally switch off from everything else. Bliss.' Amber

Here we see Amber pampering herself. Do not forget to look after yourself

Inspiration

There is a therapy in America led by a woman called Cassandra Light, who has written a book about the art and craft of personal transformation. Cassandra Light works with people who have suffered trauma by involving them in an artistic process creating sculpture. As someone is creating their sculpture, they talk about their experiences and they find that, somehow the process of producing their sculpture releases the inner pain of their past.

Working together in a creative space, people will share a common vision. The participants share stories and mutually support one another. This is one of the best ways a person can heal; to have the support of individuals who are on the journey with you and shared similar pain can be a journey into healing.

> ➤ You might like to make a collage in the journal about how you are feeling

> ➤ Then you might like to make a collage about how you would like to feel

 **It helps to focus on a hobby and have something to aim for, like painting a picture, or making something. It is the time spent in the creative process that can inspire some people. You become absorbed in the activity and this can keep your spirits up. It is also a great way to meet people.**

'Do not say it is too late'

Suzuki Roshi

At some point many people will give up. Their suffering can overwhelm them. There are those who do not make progress.

Here is a thought about personal energy by Martha Graham. It suggests that each person is unique and has fantastic potential – an inner potential to succeed, a fulfilment of who you are. All that needs to happen is for it to be recognised and then released.

It is profoundly encouraging.

'There is a vitality, a life force, an energy that is translated through you into action. And because there is only one of you in all time, this expression is unique. If you block it, it will never exist through any other medium. The world will not have it.

'It is not your business to determine how good it is, nor how valuable, nor how it compares with other expressions. It is your business to keep it yours, clearly and directly, to keep the channel open.'

Martha Graham

CREATIVE

We all possess the ability to be creative. We all have natural talent. You can be creative if you set yourself some new goals. You can be creative if you try to use your imagination in any field you choose. It can be used to design something or solve a problem.

'I thought being creative had to mean making something or painting. I've always made up stories to amuse the kids – little poems and songs – and one day my friend heard me telling them a story. She was really impressed and said I was really creative. I hadn't thought of it like that before.' Amber

---

Creative ideas that might encourage you might be:

- ➢ Writing poetry
- ➢ Painting a picture
- ➢ Life drawing
- ➢ Trying candle making
- ➢ Making furniture
- ➢ Gardening
- ➢ Mosaic work
- ➢ Sculpting
- ➢ Make a collage from photographs of your family & friends

- ➢ Making Christmas decorations
- ➢ Building a play house for children
- ➢ Making puppets for children
- ➢ Showing children how to make potato pictures
- ➢ Making a picture from dried flowers
- ➢ Decide to enrol on a college course of your choice

Making a collage or healing picture

You may wonder why this would be worth doing. You just need to try it out. You might feel down and despondent. When you feel low it might help to start to think about the collage, or gathering things to start making it. Better still is to start making one.

If you make something, you are using your hands, and this can be positive. You might like to think about the positive thoughts that you might feel about your life. In a collage you may find colours and items that can help express that.

➢ Items you may need are: paper, glue, scissors, canvas, ribbons, swatches of fabric, magazine pictures, photographs, sequins, braid, shells, paints, glitter and anything else that you may wish to use.

➢ 'I made my collage reluctantly. After a while I placed in the centre my most precious dreams. Then I placed the strong hopeful things in my life. I used blue objects for that part. Around the edge I placed a cord that linked up all the support I had in my life. I used a rich aubergine colour there. In various corners I placed the high and low points of my life. I used sand, fabric, jewellery and velvet. I found old bits and pieces to create texture. I was worried that my family might ask questions about my picture.

➢ 'I needn't have been worried. When people ask I say it is an abstract. If I want to explain I do, if I do not, I don't. I am glad I did the picture. It helped me express my life in some order as I see it. I did find it cathartic and healing. The abuse was not centre stage. I can move on from that now.' Amber

➢ 'My aim in making a collage was to enjoy it and celebrate my life. I wanted images that spoke to me of joy. I wanted to remember the happy times. I spent time finding positive images that I could use. Laughter is a great healer. I worked hard to feel positive and put lots of colour in the picture. It was successful in helping me appreciate all that was good about my life.' Raoul.

CHAPTER 10

THE HEALING JOURNEY

It might seem obvious after all that has already been written in this book that you need to heal from the damage that has been done to you emotionally and psychologically. Any physical wounds undergo the body's natural healing process.

The emotional and psychological wounds that sexual abuse and violence cause can be lifelong problems. You may have an awareness that there has been a psychological impact because of the trauma, but you put these thoughts to the back of your mind in an attempt to make yourself believe that you have not been affected or scarred by the trauma. It can be deeply distressing to believe that your mind has been affected.

There may even be a feeling of shame that you have been somehow damaged by your experiences, and that you are not as 'strong' or as 'worthwhile' as people as those who have had 'normal' experiences.

The healing journey

In fact, you might have spent a lot of time wondering and worrying about whether you are 'normal' – with you deciding more often than not that you cannot be normal – because of what has happened to you, because of how you have reacted, because of how you feel about yourself.

Some survivors always have an understanding that they have been affected by traumatic experiences, and they make allowances for themselves and take extra care of themselves in order to counteract this. You may cope well in day-to-day life, but if you have to think about the abuse or something reminds you of it, then your reactions are exactly the same as someone who has not connected their abuse experiences to the ongoing problems in their emotional and personal lives.

Many survivors will recognise that moment when there is a sudden realisation that they have to face up to traumatic experiences from the past because whatever is going wrong in their lives is linked in some way to the trauma. There are some common scenarios that can lead you to start to question what is happening in your life:

> ➢ A powerful trigger, to recognising that you have to do something to heal from trauma, is when a child in your family reaches the same age as you were when you were abused

> ➢ The death of an abuser is also a powerful trigger to remembering, especially if there was never a confrontation or open acknowledgement of the abuse

> ➢ The birth of a child, your own or a friend's, may act as a powerful reminder of the vulnerability of children –including yourself as a child

> ➢ Your own child disclosing that they have been abused

> ➢ Revictimisation – sadly, someone who has experienced abuse is more likely to experience a second or more assaults as an adult, including domestic violence. This can uncover childhood memories of abuse

> ➤ Getting into a serious relationship with a partner can trigger issues around trust and safety

> ➤ A sexual relationship can trigger flashbacks, when being touched in particular ways acts as a reminder of sexual abuse or rape

> ➤ The police or social services may make contact with a survivor in cases where there are many victims and this can cause distress

> ➤ Some survivors of rape attacks seek immediate support and counselling, although there is often a stronger wish to forget what has happened and concentrate on other things

> ➤ Survivors of rape attacks may soon find that their relationships are affected, and this leads them to the decision that they must seek out support`

We can now look at what the healing journey might be like. We have called it a journey because it may be a lengthy process, and there may be times when someone has to go back over the same ground in order to clear up their thinking or beliefs.

There are recognisable stages on the journey, and at the centre we have placed our vision for the future. Don't get discouraged if you find you've gone round the circle a few times.

It takes a while to get the hang of anything new, and changing beliefs and attitudes that have been built up over a period of time (years, sometimes) is going to be hard work! And, of course, anytime you feel low in the future you're more likely to feel that you're back at the beginning. You may feel down, but at least now you know the way back and how to get going on the journey.

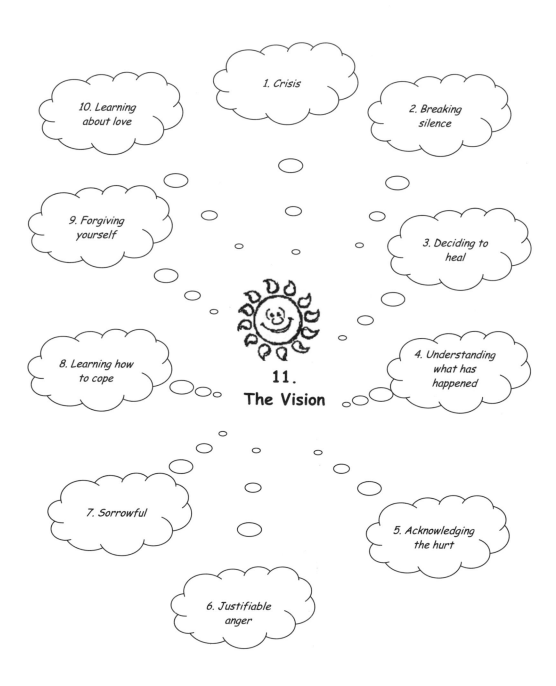

1. Crisis

10. Learning about love

2. Breaking silence

9. Forgiving yourself

3. Deciding to heal

8. Learning how to cope

11. The Vision

4. Understanding what has happened

7. Sorrowful

5. Acknowledging the hurt

6. Justifiable anger

1. CRISIS

The mind plays the event back over and over again....

- No-one will believe me
- I will always be dirty
- I am damaged
- I have never been loved
- I can never be whole
- I have been robbed of my innocence
- I feel devastated
- All my hopes have been smashed

Our message for the 'crisis' stage of the healing journey:

- You are worth bothering about
- You can feel better
- Your reactions are normal
- You are not going mad
- It's not your fault
- You are innocent
- These feelings will pass

Memories, thoughts and feelings around the abusive experience are triggered for some reason. Everywhere you look there seems to be more evidence and reminders of rape or sexual abuse in the world generally. Your feelings can seem obsessive and out of control. Mood swings are common. Nightmares, flashbacks and panic attacks can often increase at this time as well.

The healing journey

The immediate reaction to trauma or a realisation of the consequences to rape or abuse, physical or mental, can produce a dramatic experience that is like an explosion.

You may feel many conflicting emotions. You will then react accordingly. This realisation can occur at any time in your life when you realise that someone has taken advantage of you.

This can occur in an unexpected moment of discovery, that what you are experiencing is related back to traumatic experiences. It can be set off by a television programme, a book, a magazine or a film. In this moment it is like a reliving of the trauma.

The emotion is like a chain binding you to the event

You may be moved mentally to produce physical effects such as feeling physically dizzy, sweaty, or maybe suffering from hot and cold shivers. In this sort of anxiety there can be literally wave upon wave of tension. Possibly not eating or sleeping, feelings of panic, that you can't sleep because somehow you feel discovered, as if everyone knows! People often feel like they are going mad at this stage, unable to stop their minds constantly reliving the trauma.

This is when you first begin to deal with the abuse. You may feel that your life has been thrown into utter chaos. You may feel obsessed with abuse issues, and even feel that you are going crazy. It may be that suicide has crossed your mind.

Whilst this is an extremely distressing time, it is important for you to remember that it can be regarded as a stage in the healing process and it will not go on forever.

Someone who has been sexually abused or raped may feel these responses are unique to them, and you need to understand that these effects are the normal human responses to emotional trauma.

Flashbacks

Panic attacks can occur with powerful flashbacks replaying the event in the mind.

Each time this happens, your mind replays the event and it goes deeper into the unconscious. There are good reasons why the mind has been programmed to store traumatic memories differently to non-traumatic memories – this is survival we're talking about. In the distant past it was vital for human beings to be able to recognise danger and take themselves away from dangerous situations.

Therefore, when something traumatic or dangerous happens, the brain is programmed to flood with chemicals that imprint every detail of that memory – in vivid detail – colour, sound, sights, tastes, smells, emotions. Every aspect of that memory is faithfully recorded.

But, further than that, it also programmes the brain to repeat this memory instantly as soon as the same or a similar danger is perceived. This is the physical and physiological basis for flashbacks. Unfortunately, this programming works against us when the danger has passed and we no longer need to be primed and on red alert. This is when flashbacks happen constantly, as in post-traumatic stress disorder.

The healing journey

Because the memories have been recorded linking in with all the senses, it can be difficult to work out exactly what is triggering the flashbacks – is it a smell, or a sound, or is it something that has been seen out of the corner of the eye? All of these things, or combinations of sensations, can trigger someone into reliving a traumatic experience.

The bad news is that flashbacks can be persistent and can even happen more often when you start talking about traumatic experiences. But, don't let this deter you from talking through your experiences. The more you desensitise yourself to the trauma, the less intimidating and persistent the flashbacks will become. The more in control you will feel and the less frightened. The good news is, that this means that you aren't going crazy when you keep getting flashbacks for no apparent reason – there will be a trigger somewhere.

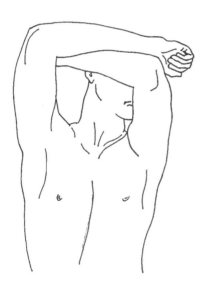

When flashbacks keep happening, the problem can be that the unconscious mind then goes into overdrive. It says, 'This is the sort of person you are, a person who this happens to. You must be going mad'.

This is nonsense, but we believe it. Yes, deep down we feel weakened, shaken, so we think it must because of something we have done. This is not true. Many people blame themselves needlessly.

If you are suffering from flashbacks, it might help you to know that the mind is more powerful than you might imagine. Uncontrolled, with no discipline, it can replay the events over and over again. But, traumatic memories can be overlaid with new, non-traumatic decisions. This takes time and effort.

What to do if you have a flashback:

➢ Ground yourself

➢ Decide what helps you to recover after a flashback, whether its something soothing or something to reconnect you to the world. You might want a warm drink, a hug from a friend, or to just sit quietly. Some people prefer to bring themselves back into today through using another sensation – biting on a lemon or smelling something pungent. Talk this through with someone close, if you can. They may want to help, but not know what to say or do. Will it help if they talk to you or give you space? Do you want to be cuddled, or do you need to be alone for a while? Find out what works best for you

➢ If you sense a flashback starting, tell yourself what is happening. 'I am having a flashback. The memories cannot harm me now. I am safe'

➢ Don't fight the flashback – often this will only delay or prolong the flashback. Let it wash over you

➢ Can you identify what may have triggered the flashback?

➢ Give yourself time to recover from the flashback

➢ Write down the flashback, or draw an image telling what was happening

➢ Tell yourself that the flashback is your way of letting go of the pain

RESOURCEFUL

You can draw on your own strength. If you feel you can't, then draw on the resources in this book. There are in the text many survivors' experiences. This book has had many stories of courage incorporated into it. Others who have survived many painful moments have been able to help others. So you can do the same.

 *Create your own action plan for coping with flashbacks*

BRAVE

You have been brave. You have fought the bad times and survived. We all need to be brave at times when we could lose hope and hide away. In going forward we need to believe we are worth it. Consider those amazing stories of courage that you hear about where someone has undergone a terrible ordeal and lived to tell the tale and gone on to achieve great success. How do they do it? The answer is they do it themselves. It is possible for someone to work at it on their own - to build up their own confidence in themselves. But, for many people, there is a need for someone else to help them see the strength they have within them, and the abilities they have to help themselves to heal.

Thinking about suicide

Some people might be thinking about suicide.

99% of all people have felt at some time like ending it all, and this doesn't mean you're going mad. It's a normal way of reacting to distressed lives. It's like the words of the musical 'Stop the world, I want to get off.'

People who feel down and want to end it all are generally people who have lost their connection to other people. In some people's experiences they might consider that people in general are all horrible. We hope to show that this is not the case and that asking for help can be the first step to rebuilding a new life.

Nothing can change what has happened. What you need to do is change how you think and feel about yourself.

Where the disappointment increases is if people who are turned to for support do not help. In some cases you might not be believed, or the person you tell makes a value judgement. The greatest problem would be if the chosen person you confide in, for whatever reason, doesn't believe you. The feelings of self-doubt and loss of self-esteem can be tremendous. This will be especially bad if it is a member of your own family you have chosen to trust.

The healing journey

Survivors sometimes find that an organisation or tradition, like the church or cultural beliefs, might speak about things like sin and not being pure, or loss of innocence and being devalued. In many traditions the loss of a person's virginity is seen as being a devaluing experience.

It might take many years to realise that the people who thought like that were actually wrong. The problem here is the amount of time invested in other people's negative views of you.

We have to mention here that male suicide is on the increase. It would seem that the male is less able to cope with extreme stress.

The trauma of an abusive situation stays with them long after the event and they need to talk about how they feel. It is not the case that a couple of sessions with a counsellor can sort out a person's feelings. Every person is different. What others need to know is that society is just recognising that the male ego is more fragile than the female, but has put very little in place to help deal with it.

The male survivor can benefit from support sessions in a group or one to one. Men can develop and move on by working on bonding with others in a group. Sadly, when one hears of the suicide rate, it appears some men are out there all alone without reaching support or help.

The wish for someone to end their life might be a consequence of some people just wanting the pain to stop as soon as possible, rather than wanting to die. They simply can't see how to stop the pain.

This is why this book is an attempt to reach those who might be out there alone who might need support. If it was possible for anyone who was feeling suicidal to know that there existed a way forward rather than assume that no help exists, then it might be that they would not consider their only option to be suicide.

Some survivors find that, by the time they have found a support service, they have already embarked upon a journey towards self-healing. The question of living and wanting to live is a discovery. It is a conscious decision to find the positive, every day in our lives.

218

Our message for people who are in the 'crisis' stage of their healing journey:

> ➤ If you are feeling suicidal, you need to realise that change is possible. Tomorrow is a different day, you are capable of changing your mind about things. Yes, it does help to talk to someone. The strongest advice is that there is an alternative to killing yourself. You must believe that there is hope and you can survive

> ➤ It has been suggested that people who kill themselves no longer see themselves as having a positive connection to others in the world. There must be someone who you can reach out to, if you do not know anyone personally then you can call the Samaritans day or night – 0800 909090

> ➤ It is very easy to say to someone that there is a reason for living, but negative experiences cannot be diminished. However, to end your life is a negative decision. What we are trying to say is that there is another way. And it might be very simple. You can find something wonderful just walking out of your door – like in nature, or the sun shining on water. The essence of being alive is the most powerful thing and most people in the world cling to that. That is a reason for living in itself

> ➤ There are people who you can talk to who will help. In the very simplest things a human being can change their whole being. Simply smiling can actually alter the whole chemical structure of your being to feel better. Going for a walk; getting a pet; listening to a piece of music; watching fish swimming in a tank - all of these things actually change your body chemistry. In these simple things, life-enhancing experiences can be found that will counteract the negative

> ➤ Hope comes from knowing that you can take control of your life and start to make your own choices and plans

CALM

When things get difficult it helps to get things under control and stay calm. Some suggestions for relaxation time include playing soft music, or relaxing in the garden. There are meditation techniques to calm yourself down. Go and make yourself a nice cup of tea; have a chocolate; light the candles and have a relaxing bath; if possible have a massage. Talking things over with a friend helps. We need to calm down by literally imagining that the problems are being let go. Some suggest meditation as a good technique to do this. You will need patience to take things slowly.

The biggest problem for people is that maybe things didn't turn out the way they hoped, and they spend a lot of time thinking 'Well, why did this happen to me? I wanted nice things to happen, and they never did.' You might realise that your own experiences could be the basis of help and inspiration for someone else. By sharing your suffering you can give hope and encouragement to another person and hopefully uplift them.

Summary

Your reactions are normal

- ➢ You are not going mad
- ➢ It's not your fault
- ➢ You are innocent
- ➢ These feelings will pass
- ➢ You can feel better

 *How could you use your experiences to help someone else?*

_____

_____

_____

_____

_____

_____

_____

_____

_____

2. BREAKING SILENCE

I have to tell someone:

> ➢ I am haunted by the memories of past experiences
>
> ➢ I know I have to tell someone
>
> ➢ Who can I tell? Who will believe me?
>
> ➢ What if it all goes wrong?
>
> ➢ How will others react?
>
> ➢ Everyone will know my secret
>
> ➢ I will be judged by everyone
>
> ➢ I'll never feel good about myself

Our message for the 'breaking silence' stage of the healing journey:

> ➢ Breaking silence is the first step in taking back control
>
> ➢ It opens up the way for healing to start
>
> ➢ The burden of secrecy is lifted
>
> ➢ Partners and friends can be supportive and caring
>
> ➢ This is the start of acknowledging you are not to blame

This stage brings with it the realisation that something has to be done to change what is happening in a person's life. This is probably the biggest step a survivor has to take, and involves the biggest realisation – that your life has been affected by trauma and that you may need help to sort this out.

We must also realise that for some people the process begins in a far less dramatic or clear way. They want to go forward in a more positive way but are unsure how to proceed and would not say that they were being healed or making a great decision to go forward.

They simply have to talk to someone. Their words may either spill out at any time, or to someone they have carefully chosen.

For some people this is far more dramatic. They know they want help to make changes and they want to talk to the police, a therapist, counsellor or doctor right away.

Where do we start?

As often happens, people have no preparation for life's tragedies. Misfortune occurs in a person's life and they are ill prepared. Here are some examples of when someone has had a bad experience and needs to tell someone else. If someone has been hurt they may feel all sorts of emotions and then decide they need to tell someone.

They might never acknowledge this to themselves. What they may do is be disruptive or exhibit other behaviour. Years later they may say that they felt badly and behaved like a troubled child. They may feel angry and let down that no-one asked them about their feelings. This is because they felt they could never tell anyone. They might have felt that if they did they might not be believed.

Disclosure can go wrong

Yet, it may be that they make a poor judgement here and choose the wrong person to disclose to. It might be someone who does not have the skills or ability to deal with what the person is telling them. It can be very traumatic for someone to have plucked up the courage to tell someone finally and then find that in doing so it can be a negative experience.

Disclosure to mothers

We mention mothers here specifically because in many instances it is a man who has abused a child, whether a father, or father figure, or other male family member. However, mothers are often blamed for not noticing, or not taking action to protect a child.

It has happened that some mothers are unable to cope when their child discloses that they have been abused. It might be that because of the mother's involvement with the abuser, it is too traumatic for them to cope with and they just blot it out. For some mothers, the disclosure by their child of sexual abuse will place them in a very difficult situation because their world can be turned upside down. They have to cope with their own feelings towards their husband/father who is possibly the abuser, and it will largely depend upon strength of character and background of the mother as to how they will cope with this.

Some mothers may find it difficult to face up to the fact that their child has been abused, fearing the consequences of losing their marriage, partner and children.

Even when the children become adults, it is really common for mothers not to accept or want to believe that their partner has abused their child or children. This is a double heartbreak for the survivor. Not only do they have to cope with the trauma of the abuse, but also the loss of the support and caring that their mother should have shown them.

As a child, you might interpret this failure as meaning that you are not lovable or that you have done something wrong. As an adult, it is possible to step back and see that your mother was and is not able to cope. They may be weak or ill, or have a failing in their personality that prevents them from protecting their children. This is a problem in them as a person and not a measure of you.

What we can say is that it is extremely unlikely for a child to lie about being abused.

Sadly, some mothers are the abusers of their own children themselves.

It may be that some mothers are in a very difficult position because of the cultural community in which they live. They may not know who to turn to for support and out of fear will remain silent. In some cultures there is the concept of 'bad blood.' It would be unthinkable to disclose to anyone that rape or abuse had happened because shame would be brought on the family.

This means that if a child has been abused, he or she could never tell anyone because their brothers and sisters would not be marriageable if it was common knowledge. In these cultures sexual abuse exists, but is not acknowledged at all. It might be for religious, or cultural reasons that the taboo is never discussed. For the survivors in these cultural groups they may feel they have no option but to suffer in silence.

Examples of disclosure that go wrong:

> A girl who was nine decided that she had to confide to her mum that her father was abusing her. The mother did not say anything straight away, but later she told the father. The girl was punished by being sent to bed early. After this, the girl was always described as a liar and blamed for anything that went wrong. This became a pattern of behaviour in that family, with the girl's word undermined constantly through being labelled a liar. She became totally ostracised by the family on separate occasions long after she had talked to her mother.

> A person who has been abused and believes in a religious tradition will find it very difficult. If they confide to a priest that they have been abused, they may find that they have to deal with the concept of sin and this makes dealing with the original incident even more difficult. This is traumatic for believers because to some degree the concept of God is about forgiveness. However, in some religious traditions, sexual abuse is seen as one of the worst sins. There is little in religious traditions to explain that the person who has been abused is not guilty. Some Christian Churches teach about original sin and the

need for penance for sins committed. The teachings on virginal purity are still there in principle in many religious traditions. If a girl is abused before marriage then their virginity would be spoiled and no one could marry them. They are then literally considered damaged goods. They will never marry. They bring utter shame on their families and their community.

➢ A boy was abused as a child, in a home for boys. He was very young when his carers' took advantage of him. He is now grown up. Some of the boys who were at the home have reported the abuse to the authorities. In order to make a case the authorities have now come to get him to tell his story and participate in the trial. He is reluctant. He has never told his wife what happened to him. He is not sure of his own reactions to being reminded of the past in this way.

In recent times authorities have been alerted to child abuse cases. They then seek to investigate the abuse that has happened, sometimes twenty years ago. They have actually knocked on people's doors and literally opened up the past for them. For some individuals this sudden reawakening of the past has been traumatic, to say the least. They are upset. They often have tried to move on with their lives. Having to tell their story and name names can be more than they feel they can bear.

Unfortunately, you may suffer not only from the initial incident itself, but often also the aftermath.

Others' responses may leave you feeling inadequate and with low self esteem.

You think the abuse is like a secret that can be discovered about you. You may see others looking at you and feel as if they know, as if there is some sign on your forehead that tells the world that something bad has happened to you, and that you are a bad person.

The physical pain of an assault may go away, but you may suffer far more from the mental anguish. You might fear contact with other people. It might be that the person you are talking to reminds you of the abuser. You might not be confident in getting your point across because of a lack of self-confidence. It might take years for you to gain the confidence to be secure in a relationship.

It might be that you were told to keep quiet or threatened in some way if you told anyone. This means that you might have lived with the fear of the consequences of telling anyone, for many years.

The majority of adult survivors of childhood sexual abuse kept the abuse a secret in childhood and often keep up that secrecy as adults. This could reflect your own situation. You may have felt too embarrassed to tell your parents. It may be that you wanted to protect your parents that you did not say anything. It might be that your parents were the abusers. You may have been too young to be fully aware of what was really happening.

It can be that the abuse happened when you were asleep and you were woken up by it. In this case you may not be confident about your memories. Some abusers do not speak to a child while the abuse is taking place. Later they do not refer to what has happened and carry on as normal. This is really confusing for a child, and you may doubt your own memories and recollections.

Dissociation

You might have found that, during abuse, you experienced a feeling of being outside your own body. Some people remember the abuse as though they are looking down on themselves from a corner of the room – like watching a film. Others retreat inside their own minds to a place where they feel safe. Their memories may be very hazy and unclear. Being able to tell a trusted human being about what happened and how you feel is a powerful healing force.

We need to recognise that for someone to break silence about their abuse is a traumatic experience. They can feel very low as they finally feel they have to say something. People may be surprised that it has been kept silent for many years.

Our message for people who are in the 'breaking silence' stage of their healing journey:

Breaking the silence, sometimes after years of secrecy, is a massive step for anyone to take. Sometimes this can go wrong if the person who is told is unable to cope, or if disclosure is forced on someone through outside intervention.

But, speaking out can also bring a wonderful release and relief. You may be surprised to find that when you do finally tell someone, maybe your partner or a friend, that you will be met with a loving response. You may also be surprised to find out that others will not judge you, but will want to show their caring and support.

Breaking silence is the first step that all survivors make in taking back control over their lives. It is a positive act, even when outside authorities make first contact, because it acknowledges that something has been done to someone that has caused hurt. It opens up the way for healing to start. It names what the possible cause of many problems has been, and allows you to start thinking about what you can change to improve your life. As the burden of secrecy is lifted, it is the start of believing you are not to blame.

Summary:

- ➤ Breaking silence is the first step in taking back control, it opens up the way for healing to start

- ➤ The burden of secrecy is lifted

- ➤ Partners and friends can be supportive and caring

- ➤ It is the start of acknowledging you are not to blame`

How would you react if your friend told you they had been abused as a child? How would you support them? What would you say to them?

3. DECIDING TO HEAL

I know I have to heal my emotional and psychological wounds:

> ➤ I have to do something to change my life

> ➤ I can't stand the pain of going on like this

> ➤ All my relationships fail

> ➤ I want to feel better about myself

Our message for the 'deciding to heal' stage of the healing journey:

> ➤ Deciding to heal is an active and positive choice

> ➤ Healing involves being prepared to accept that changes will have to be made

> ➤ You can move backwards and forwards on the road to healing

It may be that, after breaking silence, you do not feel the need for further counselling or therapy. Not all survivors experience problems of such severity that their lives are disrupted to the point where they feel they must seek support.

But, usually all survivors will benefit from the opportunity of talking to someone or finding a support group, self-help pack or website, where they can explore their beliefs and feelings about what has happened to them.

When a survivor makes the decision that they feel they must heal their psychological and emotional wounds, this comes from the realisation that things are going wrong in their lives somehow. Maybe relationships don't work out, they may have outbursts of temper or feel unable to trust anyone. They may feel that 'everything' in their lives seems to go wrong. They may be suffering from depression and suicidal thoughts and try to deal with all this with negative coping strategies.

FREEDOM

I want to be free from anything that is holding me back. I want to be free from self-doubt that might hinder my progress. I want to be free to be able to make choices. My freedom to develop is very important to me.

Many survivors will say that they find it difficult to trust anyone. So the first task In any supporting situation is to establish a solid basis for trust with the counsellor/therapist/support worker. The fact that this isn't easy will be obvious to you. The counsellor is there to focus on traumatic experiences, and the work will inevitably be painful. However, if you feel that you cannot build a trusting relationship with someone who is in a helping or supporting role, then it is your right to seek and request help from someone else.

You may say, 'How can someone who feels anguish heal themselves?' It is possible. It can be that you feel positive one minute and down the next. Little by little, you have to believe in small steps. If you rebuild the way you think, you can make significant changes in your life.

Our message for people who are in the 'deciding to heal' stage of their healing journey:

Deciding to heal involves you accepting that you are going to have to face up to painful memories. This happens when you recognise the effects of sexual abuse in your life and make an active decision to heal. The choice is to make positive steps towards the healing process and to be willing to accept the changes that will go with it.

Healing is not a single destination. It is a long process. It is not a linear process. You can move backwards and forwards on the road to healing.

Some survivors will choose to work through their painful experiences on their own. They may choose to use helplines or books as a way of healing from their experiences.

Specialist support

If you are looking for a specialist support service then we would recommend that you contact Directory and Book Services to obtain a copy of their National Directory of Rape and Sexual Abuse Support Services. The Directory lists all the agencies and services available throughout the country and gives details of their contact numbers and opening hours.

Contact DABS:

01709 860023

www.dabsbooks.co.uk

The Directory also contains useful advice on choosing a counsellor or support group.

Summary:

- ➢ Deciding to heal is an active and positive choice
- ➢ Healing involves being prepared to accept that changes will have to be made
- ➢ You can move backwards and forwards on the road to healing

 *What has decided you to heal now? What changes do you need to make for healing to happen?*

_____

_____

_____

_____

_____

_____

_____

_____

_____

_____

4. UNDERSTANDING WHAT HAS HAPPENED

➢ Even though I know in my head it wasn't my fault, I still feel guilty

➢ I should have said 'No.' It must be my fault

➢ I feel totally ashamed, as though my body betrayed me

➢ Sometimes it was me who approached the abuser. Even though I didn't like it, somehow I felt special

➢ I craved the attention. No-one else ever showed me any affection

➢ I enjoyed the money and presents that I was given

➢ I felt as thought I should have stopped it but I did not

➢ I felt ashamed I had an orgasm

Our message for the 'understanding what has happened' stage of the healing journey:

➢ It is never the victim's fault

➢ Try to be patient. It will take you time to rebalance your beliefs and thoughts about what has happened

➢ Knowing about normal responses to trauma and abuse can help to banish shame and guilt

➢ You can still have an idea of what home and family life and society should be like, no matter what negative experiences you have had

➢ Perfection is impossible, but we all deserve the opportunity to strive towards our ideals and to feel we are complete

CLEANSED

This can come from your own sense of self-help. The aim is to feel restored in spirit and not defeated. This programme is to try to uplift the spirit and hopefully cleanse you from the self-doubt that you may have had.

It is at this point in the healing journey that you begin to be in a position to think in a different way about what has happened to you.

You are ready to begin to accept being let down by people and a society that should have protected you, rather than blaming yourself or punishing yourself. You are also ready to acknowledge that in this life there can be no guarantees that anyone can be totally protected all the time.

Many survivors say they understand in their mind that they didn't do anything wrong and that they aren't to blame for what has happened. But, they still can't shake the feeling that they are dirty and guilty despite that. Partly this is because they have told themselves so often that they are to blame that it has become an automatic response for them. In fact, in any situation in general life, they may feel responsible and guilty even when they know they aren't.

Connecting up the knowledge in your mind with the feeling in your heart can take a long time. The well-worn thought pathways have to be rerouted along different lines time and time again before the belief really starts to sink in. Feelings of being dirty and ashamed will gradually start to fade as the old ways of thinking are overlaid with new ones.

What is happening is that, after acknowledging the hurt that has been done to you, it becomes possible to start to think about what your life should have been like.

All of us have the ability to develop in our minds our own idea of a perfect way of life what mothers and fathers should do to take care of children, what partners should be like in a relationship, how children should be treated with love and care, how a responsible person behaves towards others and society.

It is only when you have fixed in your mind what your goals and ideals are, that you have any chance of aiming for them.

And it is only when you have been able to acknowledge how your life and personality have been damaged through trauma that you are able to start believing you too can have goals and ideals to aim for, without punishing yourself for not being there already.

 **Active: You must try to be active, maybe doing something to help. Just sitting around will not be helpful. Think about what active means. Can you be active? If you are active physically, it will help your mental wellbeing. At its simplest level it might mean that you need to go outside and go for a walk. It's necessary to be doing something. Are you actively engaged in this process of self-awareness?**

If you are a survivor of child sexual abuse, find a picture of yourself at the age you were when the abuse started to happen. Look at the photograph. Remind yourself of how vulnerable you were at that age. Sometimes, this painful knowledge is needed to help release feelings of shame and guilt.

Many survivors experience destroying levels of shame and guilt because of how they reacted to the abuse, or because of how they see their role in what happened.

While children are not ready emotionally or physically for sexual relationships, their bodies still respond to sexual touching – all this means is that their bodies are functioning normally. Girls may find that their vaginas become lubricated and they may orgasm. Boys may find that their penis becomes erect and they may ejaculate.

Their bodies may simply be responding to being touched in a sexual way or these responses may also be due to a fear reaction. In both cases, the body is responding normally to the release of adrenalin. It means nothing more than that they have a normal, human body. What it doesn't mean is that they wanted the abuse to happen, or that they 'enjoyed' it in the true, adult, mutual way a sexual relationship is enjoyed.

SECURITY

Many survivors will say that they find it difficult to trust anyone, so the first task in any supporting situation is to establish a solid basis for trust with the counsellor/therapist/support worker. The fact that this isn't easy will be obvious to you. The counsellor is there to focus on traumatic experiences, and the work will inevitably be painful at times. However, if you feel that you cannot build a trusting relationship with someone who is in a helping or supporting role, then it is your right to seek and request help from someone else. .

Sadly, for some children the only time they are shown any affection is when they are being abused. This can cause great inner conflict, because on the one hand they do not want to be abused, but on the other they crave the affection and kindly words. Children need to experience love as much as they need shelter, food and warmth. For children, love and affection are survival needs that they need to seek out where they can.

Some families face hardships that make it difficult for parents to cope with their children, and although they would not wish them harm, they are unable to show them the love and the affection they need. A child from such a family may be vulnerable to abuse from someone outside the family.

The healing journey

There are also children who are beaten and threatened to stop them telling anyone they are being abused, and who live in fear that they or someone in their family will be harmed if they don't comply.

Raoul's Story

You may remember that Raoul was a young man who had been abused. The physical wounds had healed in a few weeks. The trauma continued in his life, as he felt less confident in making decisions. He found out that lots of people abandoned him. They said they did not like his attitude.

'As time went on, I was stealing to fund my drug habit and eventually I was caught by the police and sent to jail.

'In prison, it was not easy for me. I was a young boy, and stronger inmates racially abused me where I had to fight to protect myself. I was aware of many of the dangers that faced me in the prison. However, on one day I was caught off guard and found myself alone with two other inmates, who said I had been getting above myself and needed teaching a lesson. I was held down by one and raped by the other.

'I faced the hardest time in my life. My self-esteem was very low. I was very ashamed and I did not tell anyone in the prison what had happened to me. I struggled with self-doubt and felt that my entire life was a failure. It seemed, for as long as I could remember that people had been treating me unfairly. I needed to survive. I needed to get out of prison. I had to get away from the drugs and find a new life for myself.'

Raoul was not prepared to give up so easily, but throughout his life he would need encouragement and support. We shall see that Raoul does manage to build up his self-esteem and go forward, despite all the negative experiences that he had endured as a child and then as a young man. Raoul found a support centre and now works for the social services.

'I will admit I have been difficult with others during my life and found it hard to get on with people.'

'There were times when I was timid and suffered embarrassment, as the male is supposed to be resilient. Once I had understood that the healing process began with my own attitude towards my own feelings, then things looked brighter. I found a support group and there I was given the confidence to develop ways of coping and moving on. Now I feel I can join you in offering you a way forward.' Raoul.

Normal response to fear

The body's natural response to any traumatic stimulus is always the same – every single system in the body is put onto red alert so that it is ready to respond immediately to whatever event is happening. This is generally known as the 'fight or flight reflex'.

All the body's systems are shocked into activity in this way, all of our automatic instinctive behaviours are triggered. The body doesn't know whether to fight, faint, run away, find food, go into shock, move its bowels or even have sex.

What is happening is that the brain has been flooded with chemicals, including adrenalin, pumping up the heart rate and increasing the body's sensitivity to all sensations.

What this means is that when a woman is in a traumatic situation, she may experience arousal of any of these systems, including the reproductive system, and that can lead to the physical response of an orgasm during rape even though she feels frightened and violated. A woman's body will often also release an egg at this time, which results in many people who are raped becoming pregnant.

Similarly, in a traumatic situation a male may get an erection and ejaculate, even though he is experiencing fear and disgust at the same time.

It is important for some survivors to know that if their bodies have responded by becoming aroused when they have been sexually assaulted, then this is a normal fear response.

Some survivors have felt guilty and ashamed of these responses for many years when the knowledge of the normal fear responses would have freed them from these damaging emotions.

When someone has been raped they often experience very similar feelings to those of someone who has been sexually abused as a child. Feelings of self-blame and doubt, feeling dirty and guilty. There may be the total destruction of someone's confidence and they may feel worthless and as though their life has no value any more.

Sadly, re -victimisation is something that many survivors of childhood sexual abuse experience. This means that they are more likely as adults to have experienced a further abusive attack. Their feelings that they must be at fault become even more ingrained.

It is a 'decision' by the abuser to commit the crime of rape or sexual assault. They have often planned what they are going to do, and are determined to carry out the attack. The victim is often someone they know either closely, or as an associate. In our legal system, this 'decision' does not define an abuser as being insane. They are seen as having the ability to 'choose' to break the law.

But where does this leave the survivor? How can anyone understand someone choosing to hurt another, by raping or sexually abusing them? The acts themselves are incomprehensible.

Our minds reject this apparent paradox – how can someone be sane and yet commit a violent act? The solution to this dilemma for many survivors can be to decide that you must have done something to cause the attack. You shouldn't have upset your partner, you shouldn't have gone out for a drink, you should have known better than to invite someone back to your home.

We believe that anyone who can make the choice to abuse another is actually demonstrating that they are not able to think and behave in a mentally healthy way. Whether they are categorised as criminals or insane, their actions mean that they are not making rational choices.

This understanding of why someone abuses others is not an easy piece of information to have – it means that there are people in the world who do harm for no other reason than that they choose to. They choose to act in supremely selfish ways to feed their own needs for control or power over another.

It is very sad that we all have to be aware that there are people in the world who are capable of hurting others in this way, and that we all have a responsibility to ourselves and others to be aware of this.

Survivors of rape attacks need this knowledge to start to free themselves from punishing blame about why they have been raped. They also need to build up their belief that there are good people in the world who are caring and selfless.

Our message for people who are in the 'understanding what has happened' stage of their healing journey:

How can anything be a victim's fault? This seems obvious, but we often think that if we had that moment to live again we would do things differently. This is called hindsight. It is a privilege survivors do not have.

Understanding how the human body responds to abuse and trauma can allow you to start to think and feel differently about yourself and how you reacted. This can then develop your understanding of how you have been betrayed. Now you can work with this knowledge to the belief that you were not to blame in any way.

The healing journey

If you've spent lots of time telling yourself that you're a bad person or not worth bothering about, then it's going to take time to counteract that. This is why we have to stress that it is never the victim's fault. When bad feelings start, tell yourself that you are bound to feel this way but that you will feel better.

There is a balance needed in how we perceive what the world is like. We all need to keep safe – watching out for our families and friends, making sure we follow simple safety rules when we are out and about – keeping in groups, trusting our instincts.

But we also need to hold onto our ability to believe in the good that is in the world around us.

Although perfection is never possible, we can all strive towards our ideals. If you have never experienced what a good family and home life can be like, then take time to imagine what you would like it to be like. This is what you deserve.

Summary:

➢ It is never the victim's fault

➢ It may take a lot of time for you to rebalance beliefs and thoughts about what has happened

➢ Knowing about normal responses to trauma and abuse can help you to banish shame and guilt

➢ We can all have an idea of what home and family life and society should be like

➢ Perfection is impossible, but we all deserve the opportunity to strive towards our ideals

---

INSIGHT

Your experiences in life have hopefully given you an insight into the depths of the spirit. It will be up to you to decide how far you will go towards using the insight that you have gained in the future.

242

How do you believe family life should be? If you had an unhappy childhood, then maybe you have seen a happy childhood portrayed in a film or book. This will give you ideas to help you to visualise what childhood can be like. Whilst you cannot experience this for yourself, you can offer it to children around you.

What do you think a happy childhood should be like?

5. ACKNOWLEDGING THE HURT

➢ The feeling of being alone can overwhelm me

➢ I feel like I am damaged beyond repair

➢ I wish time could stand still and that bit of life could be rewound and edited out. But that cannot happen

➢ I feel a torrent of conflicting emotions

➢ What has been taken cannot be put back

➢ My self-worth and everything I believed in has gone

➢ I get frequent nightmares

➢ I suffer from panic attacks

➢ I get flashbacks

➢ I cried, and then wept until I couldn't cry any more. There are no more tears to shed

Our message for the 'acknowledging the hurt' stage of the healing journey:

➢ What has happened to you can never be rewound or edited out. No-one can alter the past

➢ Moving on to the next stage of understanding what has happened can allow you to gain a perspective on your experiences

➢ Everyone can change the way they feel about what has happened to them

➢ Everyone can change the way they feel about themselves

> ➢ Talking things through offers the chance to develop self-acceptance

> ➢ You need to know that whatever you have done to cope, and however you have survived, you have done your best

> ➢ New ways of coping can start to be considered and tried

You may have spent many years trying to put memories of abuse to the back of your mind. So the process of healing inevitably involves some aspects of remembering both incidents and feelings that you have successfully blocked out for a long time. Remembering can involve memories, flashbacks or even the physical sensations felt in your body at the time of the abuse.

Some survivors may doubt their own memory, feelings and perceptions of the abuse. They may deny that it really was that bad. Coming to believe in the reality of the abuse, and that it really hurt you, is an important part of the healing process.

As you start to think in depth about what your experiences are, then the full impact of all the after-effects becomes apparent. You may become aware of very painful realisations that relationships, family circumstances and life potential have been severely restricted or twisted. However, this is also when it will become apparent to you where the healing is needed in yourself.

Unfortunately, at this time, just when you may have started to feel a sense of relief at being able to be open about your past experiences, you may actually start to experience flashbacks, or may find that flashbacks increase dramatically.

New memories may also start to come to the surface. It can be extremely distressing to find that there are further incidents to be dealt with and coped with. Further times of being let down and betrayed.

Some survivors of childhood sexual abuse will say that they have very few memories of their childhood. In some cases, you might find that the memories will never come back – this may be the result of dissociation from painful experiences. Some survivors find that memories slowly return over a period of months, but that they may still be very vague and unclear.

If a child is abused at a very young age then they may not have had the words and understanding to store memories like an older child or adult can. Their memories may be stored in body sensations – unaccountable feelings of panic and terror, or crushing sensations, stomach or back pains or other aches and pains.

As someone tells their story, it often becomes very clear to them how their life has been affected. The negative coping strategies they may have used, and the full impact on their whole life becomes clear.

'There were times when I felt ugly and unloved. I found relationships with men difficult. Yet, as I got older, I got married and had a family. I had tried in many ways to make a success of my life. I was unhappy that my husband turned out to be aggressive and resorted to physical violence against me on occasions.

'One day I was walking home from work along a towpath beside a canal. There was a man who was sitting down near the path. As I passed he asked me for a light for a cigarette. I said I did not smoke. Then I continued along the way and then I realised that the man was following me. I became more anxious and started to run, but the man caught up with me and attacked me. He pulled me into the bushes. There the man raped and left me. I was found several hours later by a passer-by who called for an ambulance. I suffered many injuries to my face and body. Because of the traumatic experience, I found it hard to identify the attacker.

'The person who raped me was put in jail. However, for me the road to recovery was going to be a long one. The physical wounds could be healed, but it was going to take longer for the psychological scars to heal.' Amber.

Amber's experience is reflected in all people who have suffered at the hands of a stranger attacking another. Rape like this is not common. It is extremely traumatic, and the after-care a person receives is vital. In Amber's case, there was very little after-care. She was not given a counsellor, or a self-help guide, or referred on to anyone. She suffered afterwards from low self-esteem and bulimia (an eating disorder).

However, all along during that experience was the memory of what had happened to her as a younger person - that she had been sexually abused. This had not stopped her from making decisions in her life, but on many occasions it had been much harder for her to make positive choices.

She needed to talk about her lack of confidence and inner pain to someone she trusted. For many years she had never told anyone of her experiences. Later on, with help, she was able to tell family and close friends that she was a survivor of sexual abuse. This coming to terms with a traumatic past enabled her to make positive steps towards a better future. Amber later goes on to find support and develop her own sexual healing workshop for survivors.

Our message for people who are in the 'acknowledging the hurt' stage of their healing journey:

This can be a shocking and painful time of insight. Often the knowledge gained will be extremely painful to you, and care is needed in being able to soothe that hurt. Moving through this stage can allow you to begin to gain a perspective on your experiences.

Nothing can change what has happened, and there will always be painful feelings around these memories. What has happened can never be rewound or edited out. No one can alter the past. But everyone can change the way they feel about what has happened to them. And they can change how they feel about themselves after what has happened.

The healing journey

Whatever negative coping strategies you may have used, however you may have coped, and however you may have blamed yourself, there is now the chance for self-forgiveness and acceptance and to know you are doing your best.

 **Get a pet: it will change your understanding of yourself - lots of research shows that petting animals de-stresses us. They love us unconditionally. It is also a focus for you outside of yourself. It gives you someone else to care for.**

Many people find it difficult to believe that anything can alter how they feel. The main benefits of taking time to work through painful memories are that: it offers you the time and space to develop self-acceptance; and an understanding that whatever you have done to survive and whatever negative coping strategies you may have used, you have been doing your best. No one could ask you to have done any more. Now you have the chance to work out what other ways of coping might be more helpful in your life. What has happened can never be rewound or edited out. No one can alter the past.

Summary:

➢ Moving on to the next stage of understanding what has happened can allow you to gain a perspective on your experiences

➢ You can change the way you feel about what has happened to you

➢ You can change the way you feel about yourself

➢ Thinking things through offers the chance to develop self-acceptance

➢ You need to know that whatever you have done to cope and however you have survived, you have done your best

➢ New ways of coping can start to be considered and tried out

Look back to an earlier journal. In what way are your feelings different now?

If all your energy doesn't go into feeling angry or upset about abuse experiences, what is the energy used for?

6. JUSTIFIABLY ANGRY

- ➤ I am angry this has happened to me
- ➤ I am angry at myself
- ➤ I am angry at others for having a better life than me
- ➤ I want to punish the person who abused me
- ➤ My anger affects how I see everything right now
- ➤ I am angry and therefore do not cope with my feelings very well
- ➤ I have lashed out at times

Our message for the 'justifiably angry' stage of the healing journey:

- ➤ Righteous anger is a healthy and appropriate response when someone has been hurt by the deliberate actions of another
- ➤ To want revenge is a normal reaction to being hurt
- ➤ To act out revenge is illegal and harmful to everyone
- ➤ Once anger has been tamed, other emotions can be uncovered
- ➤ Fear and vulnerability may have been underlying feelings of anger, but it becomes safe to acknowledge them
- ➤ A new awareness of emotions can start to develop

RESPONSIBILITY

You have a responsibility to yourself now to do well. You need to achieve your goal of following the healing journey and this means taking responsibility for your life now.

Once an understanding of what has happened has been developed, then what you may notice is the feeling of justifiable anger against the betrayal and against what has been lost.

This is a healthy and appropriate anger, and is quite different to the rages and tempers that many survivors experience in the Crisis Stage.

What can you do with this feeling of anger? Negative ways of coping with emotions may have been deeply ingrained – like using drugs or alcohol to numb feelings or distract attention away from uncomfortable thoughts. There is a strong link between sexual abuse and rape and self-injury, and this can be connected to feelings of anger towards the self.

 **Go for a walk outside in the fresh air – even for a very short time this is beneficial. Go for a walk in the garden, a hillside, or the woods. Problems indoors can overwhelm; outside they seem less powerful. Go for a walk in the daytime.**

You have every right to feel angry about what has happened to you. What do you imagine yourself doing with that anger?

Revenge

We guess that many survivors will want their revenge on the person who has harmed them. They may have very detailed ideas of what they would like to do to pay them back for all the hurt they have caused.

We don't blame them at all. But, we do have a few things to say about it too:

> Wanting revenge – to hurt and destroy, even - someone who has been abusive is a natural response, so there's no need to feel bad, if this is how you feel

> We don't believe true inner peace can come from being vengeful

> ➢ The law will punish anyone who takes it upon themselves to try to make their own justice

> ➢ Living with a constant level of anger and hatred against someone else locks that person into the effects of the abuse

> ➢ There is no freedom in carrying thoughts of revenge; it simply chains you to the abuse experience

'I was so angry at Father Bernard. I hated him. I wanted him to suffer like me. Yet he went on to abuse others in other towns. My anger motivated me to get to a self- help group. I can never forgive Father Bernard. I learnt compassion for my own lost childhood and now I am doing something about that. Forgiveness is not something I associate with Father Bernard. He has to deal with his own conscience.' Niles

If you have overwhelming thoughts of wanting to have your revenge, what we suggest you do is to consider how you feel about this.

There are two possibilities: you could find some quiet time to sit and think through what you would actually like to do to get your revenge. If you are in a support group you could talk this through with the others. Be as inventive as you like. You may want to be cruel and violent. Remember that as long as all you do is imagine your revenge, then no one actually gets hurt, and you don't find yourself serving a life sentence for assault or worse.

The alternative is to forgive, and we discuss this later on. The only safe thing to do is to imagine your revenge, however the choice between revenge and forgiveness is yours.

One support group for survivors that we know took several sessions to talk about how they would like to get their revenge on the people that had hurt them. There were many suggestions, some of them very violent. Some were extremely inventive, like painting the word 'Paedophile' on the back of the abuser's car in neon paint and then driving after them at night shining a torch on the car. Everyone would see the message, and the abuser would be shamed without knowing why.

Lots of emotion was released, and the group enjoyed both laughter and tears as they talked. Everyone was kept grounded by reminding themselves that to want revenge was normal, to actually carry it out was illegal and would be damaging to themselves.

 Clear out everything you've been meaning to throw away and take it down to the dump. Throwing the rubbish as far as you can into the back of the dump can feel really wonderful! See if you can hit particular targets in the dump.

Different emotions

It is at this point in the healing journey that a survivor will be ready to look at the other emotions that might lie underneath feelings of anger. It has not been safe until this point to acknowledge that one of the strongest emotions can be fear – of further attacks, of being vulnerable, of what has been lost. Many survivors react with anger because acknowledging the fear that is driving that anger would make them feel too vulnerable.

After the realisation that the anger you have carried for so long has really been an expression of fear, you will be ready to take on board your emotional responses to living with anger and in fear.

New ways of expressing emotions must be learned. Sometimes, new emotions have to be recognised. If all emotions have been submerged under frustration and irritability or guilt, then different feelings can come as a shock.

'I seemed to suddenly notice one day, after I'd been talking to my counsellor for a while, that everything seemed to be more solid. I know it sounds strange, but it was like I was finally living in the present day. It was as if a veil had been lifted away and I could connect up to everything in a way that had not been possible before. I noticed little things, like the detail and colours of flowers. I can't say I felt wonderful all the time, but I felt okay.' Amber.

Be aware of your body and how your mind is feeling in your everyday life. You may not be used to asking yourself, 'How do I feel?' but start to do that today. Check out what is going on inside you.

 *Can you imagine what they feel like? How many different emotions can you name? What activity will comfort or soothe or help each emotion?*

_____

_____

_____

_____

If you feel down?

_____

_____

_____

_____

_____

If you feel lonely?

_____

_____

_____

_____

_____

Our message for people who are in the 'justifiably angry' stage of their healing journey:

> ### ANGER
>
> This is a powerful and liberating force. Whether you need to get in touch with it, or have always had plenty to spare, directing your rage squarely at your abuser, and those who didn't protect you, can be vital to healing. Justified anger is healthy and appropriate.

To want revenge is a normal reaction, but has to be managed in a positive way.

When all your emotional time and brainpower is not being taken up with angry thoughts, then it becomes possible for you to identify and discover other emotions.

We can all be vulnerable. Many survivors have lost touch with the child within themselves - their own vulnerability. Many men and women talk about being afraid to be vulnerable. But getting in touch with these feelings can be a strength not a weakness, and can help survivors to become more open to the full range of their feelings.

Righteous anger is a healthy and appropriate response when someone has been hurt by the deliberate actions of another.

Summary:

> ➢ To want revenge is a normal reaction to being hurt
>
> ➢ To act out revenge is illegal and harmful to everyone
>
> ➢ Once anger has been tamed, other emotions can be uncovered
>
> ➢ Fear and vulnerability may have been underlying feelings of anger, but it becomes safe to acknowledge them
>
> ➢ A new awareness of emotions can start to develop

If you aren't spending all your time angry, how will you feel?

_____

_____

_____

_____

_____

_____

_____

_____

_____

How do you want to feel?

_____

_____

_____

_____

_____

_____

_____

_____

_____

7. SORROWFUL

You grieve for all the lost opportunities – I could have been this, or done that, or had good relationships, if only...

> ➢ My childhood has gone
>
> ➢ I had no choice about losing my virginity
>
> ➢ I have no family
>
> ➢ I am so bitter and resentful at life
>
> ➢ Why me?
>
> ➢ I feel fit to break, like a vessel that is cracked, and cannot be repaired

Our message for the 'sorrowful' stage of the healing journey:

> ➢ Survivors have much to grieve and mourn – they have faced terrible and sometimes lasting losses
>
> ➢ At this stage, they have sufficient inner resources to start to cope with this grief
>
> ➢ Over time, grief and sadness can be released
>
> ➢ Positive experiences provide new memories to balance the unhappy memories
>
> ➢ This stage will not last forever. You will feel better

This is a difficult area. It is not the same for everyone. There was one survivor who said this: 'My life had died. My dreams had died. My future had died. My world had died.' The person was as distressed as if someone had actually died. It was dramatic at the time. What was happening was that at that moment the person felt complete despair.

After several years, that feeling started to change. The person never forgot what they experienced. What they did was to move on. The focus of their mind turned to the future.

'I do grieve for myself as a child. I wish I could tell that boy that someone cared for him. I remember crying myself to sleep. I remember the pain and trying to hide it from others. Sometimes I cried for events that had happened many years in the past.' Niles

We don't believe in the saying 'time heals everything.' In fact, we believe that at any time if you start to focus on abuse experiences and the effect it has had on you, then you will experience all the raging emotions you first experienced in the crisis stage.

What time can do though, is allow enough space for grieving to take place.

SELF-AWARENESS

We are more aware of our emotions and aware of how we feel towards suffering. We will use this to make us stronger as survivors.

If the full force of grief and sadness were to be felt all at once then there would be a sense of being totally overwhelmed. Over time, grief and sadness can be slowly released.

Tears contain chemicals that the body needs to release in order to rebalance emotions. This is why it can be healing to cry. If you have held your emotions in check for a long time, it might be difficult for you to let go enough to allow tears to flow. You might find you need to set aside time on your own to let your emotions out.

'I had to wait until the children were in bed. I could be strong in the daytime, when I was busy looking after them. But after they had settled off for the night I couldn't keep it up. I cried for hours. The slightest sad thing on TV set me off. I even cried at adverts. It was as though I was full to the brim. Once, I cried all the way through Titanic from the minute it started. Afterwards, I sat with a cup of tea. I felt cried out, but sort of satisfied as well.' Amber.

As you progress on the healing journey you are building up new ways of acknowledging and coping with different emotions. Your attitudes become much more rounded and balanced as your thoughts are able to focus on other aspects of life, other than the trauma.

As you begin to heal from the trauma, you can experience the positive things in life that sustain us all. Some of the simplest activities can be remembered with joy and happiness. Our suggestions for caring for yourself throughout this book will all provide little bonuses of good feelings. They can build up good memories to act as a balance to the sad ones.

Grieving

Grieving is a step in the process of healing. It is not something that will last for ever. Be kind to yourself while you are feeling this way, and believe that you will feel better.

Imagine that you are on that beautiful beach enjoying the experience. If you use your imagination, then it may not be exactly the same, but it can help. The imagination can stimulate the brain to enjoy an experience even if it is not real.

Our message for people who are in the 'sorrowful' stage of their healing journey:

You have much to grieve and mourn – you may have faced terrible and sometimes lasting losses. Your whole life may have been affected through the loss of your family, your childhood, your faith, your innocence and your freedom.

However, at this stage you have reached the point where you are developing a strong enough position, emotionally, to be able to withstand this grief and to take positive action to handle it.

As you feel more healed from the trauma, you can start to build up new and positive memories to balance out the sad and unhappy times.

Summary:

> ➢ At this stage, you are developing sufficient inner resources to start to cope with your sorrow and grief

> ➢ Over time, grief and sadness can be released

> ➢ Positive experiences provide new memories to balance the unhappy memories

> ➢ This stage will not last forever. You will feel better

How do you express sorrow?

_____

_____

_____

_____

_____

_____

_____

_____

What helps?

_____

_____

_____

_____

_____

_____

_____

_____

_____

8. LEARNING HOW TO COPE

'I hoped there would be a magic moment when I suddenly felt completely recovered.' Raoul

> ➢ I thought that after all this time, I would just feel better
>
> ➢ I still have awful days, when I seem to feel just as bad as ever
>
> ➢ I make mistakes
>
> ➢ When I went through a bad patch I started drinking again
>
> ➢ I've self-injured again

Our message for the 'learning how to cope' stage of the healing journey:

> ➢ Learning to cope is a new experience
>
> ➢ This is the stage when new beliefs and attitudes are reinforced through day-to-day life, that can sustain self-esteem through the bad times

> ➢ Setbacks can be upsetting, and you can find that old negative ways of coping are easier to rely on than new ways that have to be worked at
>
> ➢ Don't feel disheartened, you are still doing your best
>
> ➢ Learning to trust thoughts, feelings and perceptions forms a new basis for actions in life
>
> ➢ In recognising life has ups and downs, you can feel like you are a survivor

This stage is all about building belief in your own self-worth, in reinforcing the new attitudes and beliefs that you have been developing throughout your healing journey so far. This is the stage when you might start to think of yourself as a survivor.

There is a process of learning about using new coping strategies. Starting to make those changes that need to be made and that you choose to make. All the knowledge that has been taken on board so far is used to build up belief in your own innocence, that you did/are doing your best, and that it really wasn't your fault.

At this stage you are still learning how to live day to day, soothing the hurt you still feel, and slowly building up your sense of self-worth, as you start to react differently to life's challenges.

There will be mistakes and setbacks. There are many things in life that can cause anyone to feel distressed or angry. What can happen is that if feelings are experienced that are similar to those felt at the time abuse happened, you can re-experience those feelings in full force.

As a child you could not really know what the impact of being abused could be on your life. As an adult, you are fully aware of all the consequences. This means that feelings from childhood are amplified and magnified through an adult's understanding of consequences.

Because our bodies remember emotions in this way, then these feelings can be triggered by things that are not related directly to previous abusive experiences – a car accident, being mugged or robbed, even an argument, or feeling ignored.

If you are someone who has used alcohol or drugs to help you cope, then it can be very tempting to rely on them again when things get difficult.

If you have used self-injury as a coping mechanism, then you may find that when you become distressed, you get a very strong desire to self-injure again. The same is true for reckless behaviour and gambling. Relationships can suffer as well.

If a person feels at the edge they are incapable of making appropriate decisions. They will talk to themselves as if they are weak and vulnerable. In doing this, you can be your own worst enemy.

The healing journey

If you feel you have slipped back to old ways of coping, then think about the journey you have already made on your way to recovering. Look back over your journal and see what helped you in the past. It will help if you can see any setbacks as a way of strengthening new ways of coping. You have to come to a point where you see that you are not useless, and that inner belief can set you free.

Nobody can ever be perfect. It may be that someone has to go round the cycle of the healing journey a few times before it all starts to really make sense.

The best guide for us all in healing is our own inner voice. Learning to trust our own thoughts, feelings and perceptions forms a new basis for actions in our own life.

Our message for people who are in the 'learning to cope' stage of their healing journey:

Summary:

> There will inevitably be better and worse days, but the better days may soon start to outnumber the bad days

> The most important message is to keep going

> Be kind and patient with yourself while you are gaining your Learning to Cope skills. Don't be put off by setbacks and listen for your inner voice

> The really hard work of acknowledging and understanding the hurt has been completed. Painful emotions have been recognised and new ways of managing them have been tried out

> This all helps to build up confidence in coping and being able to make positive changes and choices

> This is the stage when new beliefs and attitudes are reinforced, in day to day life, that can sustain self-esteem through the bad times

➢ Learning to trust thoughts, feelings and perceptions forms a new basis for actions in life

➢ You can start to feel that you are a survivor

 Look in a mirror and tell yourself 'I am a survivor'. How do you feel when you tell yourself this?

9. FORGIVING YOURSELF

I can't imagine forgiving the person who did this to me:

> ➤ I can't forgive others for hurting me

> ➤ I think I should forgive because otherwise how can I move on?

Our message for the 'forgiving yourself' stage of the healing journey:

> ➤ Bad things happen – but what has happened does not have to be the most important event in your life

> ➤ Through your experiences you may find that you have developed more insight into relationships, you may have strong beliefs about protecting children and human rights, you may feel that you are more caring and compassionate than you would have otherwise have been

> ➤ Forgiving someone who has been abusive is an act of choice that you may not want and should not feel pressured to make

> ➤ Self-forgiveness involves a process of acknowledging the hurt, accepting that it belongs in the past and feeling in control of emotions and life choices

Forgiving yourself may seem a strange title for a stage in the healing journey. Many people will think it's obvious that the victim has done no wrong.

This can be a very resistant belief to remove. Part of the reason for this is that, if we are responsible for something happening, then it is also in our power to stop it happening again. If you take on the responsibility for being abused or raped, then you also take on the power to stop it. But that also means feeling guilty about it.

This is not a conscious decision, but a way of coping that comes out in your attitude towards yourself.

TOLERANT

We always admire people who are tolerant of others. This is an important quality to develop in ourselves. We may suffer from anger problems and be intolerant of others when we see their faults. However, to be sympathetic and develop tolerance is admirable.

Mae West said: 'If something is doing you harm then don't do it!' Her self-confidence and positive regard for herself shone out. She believed that thinking negative thoughts literally influenced the body.

Today we might find doctors who would agree. We have to find a way of looking to the future and not allow the past to control our minds. It is like twisting the knife of the past over and over again. When you can let go of the past you could reach a stage of moving forward and forgiving yourself, believing in your own innocence. Most survivors somehow end up believing they were to blame. Forgiving yourself and letting go of the guilt and shame allows all your energies to be used in thinking about what's happening for you today.

At this stage, you are ready to let go of your need to take on the responsibility for the abuse happening. You are developing enough self-worth and self-belief to accept that you are the innocent victim and that nothing you did would have caused or prevented the abuse.

This stage may bring a real sense of peace and inner comfort, as you let go of punishing ways of thinking about yourself and truly start to benefit from the positive changes you have been working on.

TRANQUILITY

You will feel that now you can be more calm and even tranquil, when things are seen in a positive light.

Some people believe that you have to forgive your abuser in order to heal. We don't think this is true. However, hating someone is a waste of your resources. It is better to not hold on to hate. If you do, then the person is still affecting your life. They are in some sense still hurting you, years after the event. You have to learn to deflect your attention to other things in life.

Some people have a very strong conviction that forgiveness is essential for complete healing. You don't have to believe this. For some survivors, talking about forgiveness of those who have made them suffer is impossible.

For others, their beliefs or faith tell them that forgiveness is essential. We would say that this belief is an ideal that very few people can really aspire to. If it is part of your belief system that you must forgive, then we would tell you to be gentle with yourself and accept the time it might take you to reach that point.

 **Have a favourite meal or invite friends round and cook them a meal. Go to a restaurant. Be adventuresome, try some new food. You may be surprised. Become a gourmet. Food can make lots of people happy. Try something that makes you feel better. Do something for others, for example bake cookies for kids. Show kids how to make cookies.**

To forgive is really difficult. Some people may never be able to forgive. That is their choice. However, carrying the hatred and vengeance in your heart can do you long-term damage, both physically and emotionally. It could stop you from moving forward. Only you can decide what purpose forgiving has in your healing journey - whether you feel you must forgive the person who has hurt you, or whether you recognise your need to forgive yourself.

PURITY

You can see things clearly and be pure of heart. Know that you do something because you want to do it and are not forced into it. To have a clear conscience may be a step towards feeling pure of heart.

Our message for people who are in the 'forgiving yourself' stage of their healing journey:

Sometimes we just have to accept that bad things happen.

This awful thing has happened, but doesn't have to be the biggest event of your life. Maybe it could make you:

- ➢ A kinder, more thoughtful person
- ➢ More insightful about relationships
- ➢ Want to defend Human Rights
- ➢ Never let your children experience what you have endured
- ➢ Realise that you have not suffered in vain
- ➢ More resilient

When we thought about survivors forgiving themselves, we tried to work out what that would actually mean. We believe that in order to live a life that is free from emotional chains tying you back to the past, you need to reach a stage where you can look back at the past without tormenting yourself with feelings of doubt or guilt. When you reach this stage, you may spend many weeks and months without even thinking about the trauma. Nightmares and flashbacks will be less frequent and you now have coping strategies to help you if they do happen.

If you were to concentrate on traumatic experiences, you would probably become angry and upset still, no matter how far you feel you have progressed. The familiar feelings of being betrayed and damaged could still come to the surface.

But, because of the knowledge you have gained through your healing journey, you have discovered new and different ways of coping with your feelings. New patterns of thinking and coping can increase your ability to sustain your sense of self-worth. As these new ways are used more and more often, they build up your resistance to the onslaught of damaging emotions.

We therefore came up with a three-stage process for forgiveness. Maybe not forgiveness, but 'threegiveness'[3] especially for survivors:

> You can acknowledge the hurt done

> You can also accept that it belongs in the past

> You can release the chains tying the past to the present and start to feel in control of your life and your own emotions

Summary:

> Bad things happen – but what has happened does not have to be the most important event in your life

> Through the experience you may find that you develop more insight into relationships, you may have strong beliefs about protecting children and Human Rights and, you may feel that you are more caring and compassionate than you would have otherwise have been

> Forgiving someone who has been abusive is an act of choice that you may not wish to make and you should not feel pressured to make

[3]With special thanks to Isaac Asimov who taught me the joy of puns. Fay

> ➢ 'Threegiveness' - Self-forgiveness involves a three stage process of: acknowledging the hurt; accepting that it belongs in the past; and feeling in control of emotions and life choices

> ➢ I can see a brighter future for me now

> ➢ I can move on

> ➢ I will be positive

> ➢ If it is going to happen, it is up to me

> ➢ I can find something positive in what has happened – maybe I can help others

> ➢ Maybe I can love myself and even other people

 *What are your feelings about forgiveness?*

_____

_____

_____

_____

_____

_____

_____

APPROPRIATE ASSERTIVENESS

Now you need to learn to stand up for yourself. You need to become assertive, to say what you want to happen now. If this means saying no more often than yes, then hopefully you will feel more confident about doing so.

10. LEARNING ABOUT LOVE

> ➢ I have lots of sex but never make love

> ➢ How could anyone love me?

> ➢ There are too many triggers when someone touches me

Our message for the 'learning about love' stage of the healing journey:

> ➢ Be kind to yourself while you relearn how to enjoy physical love

> ➢ Create safe foundations for sexual healing

> ➢ Build trust in yourself and your partner

> ➢ Reclaim your own body – accept how it responds and reacts to sensations

> ➢ Respect your own and your partner's needs

> ➢ Communicate – express your needs and desires, and listen to your partner

> ➢ Identify triggers and find coping strategies to meet them

> ➢ Allow yourself to develop new and joyful associations for sexual experiences

We will remember that we have already said that if a person is not able to show self-care, self-nurturing or self-love, then they will not be able to fully show these to others in their lives.

When you reach this stage in the healing journey, the truth of this will become very apparent to you. It is only when you have worked through all the other stages that you are really ready and able to start showing yourself the kind of self-care and self-love that builds lasting and emotionally nourishing self-worth and self-esteem.

CHERISH

We can cherish those we love. We can cherish the good times we have had and those still to come. We can look forward and cherish those moments that we are planning, that will be a success in the future.

You are now ready to share yourself emotionally and physically, if you choose to, with the people you love.

This is the part of the story where the hero and heroine ride off into the sunset to live happily ever after.

Of course, we all know that it's only in fiction that happy ever afters happen. Life has ups and downs, things happen, people's emotions can be affected by many different situations.

This is why we don't promise a happy ever after. What we can say is that you can live your life able to choose what you do, how you react, how you spend your time. When happiness visits, you will be able to recognise it and cherish it for what it is.

A feeling of resolution comes when feelings begin to stabilise and you begin to feel like a whole person. You are able to make some of the changes that you want in your life, developing positive relationships and begin exploring your potential as a human being.

BLESSED

At times when we are feeling down we may say there is nothing to feel blessed about. To feel blessed is to accept that there are others who have faced more difficult times than yourself.

Love

The most difficult thing in the world is to learn about love. Lots of people have sex, but they don't necessarily make love. The biggest question to ask is, 'What is love?' The word is often used, but perhaps impossible to define. Love depends on your point of view, your culture and your value system. Today it is perhaps being threatened by a very individualistic approach to life. The increased number of sexual abuse cases, including Internet porn and child porn, would seem to suggest that the idea of love is being destroyed.

Love, according to the Greeks, was defined by using different words. Today we need to teach emotional literacy in school. This is because people cannot articulate their own emotions.

There have been many incidents of physical abuse that are linked to people's uncontrolled powerful emotions. With a lack of emotional restraint, they can be totally unchecked and out of control. Some abuse stems from people's confused conflict of emotions. Some abusers may even believe that what they are doing is somehow linked to love. It seems ridiculous to have to say that love cannot be demanded by anyone. Love, if it is real, has to be reciprocal. If a person does not want the advances of someone else, it cannot be called love.

It is tragic that this has to be spelt out to children and adults almost continuously. Date rape and the spiking of people's drinks seem to suggest that people do not take it seriously. There must be some people who have committed an act of aggression to another person, who do not have any conscience that will tell them that they have done something wrong.

In the Greek understanding of agape there is the idea of a general love for humanity. When explained to children in school they react with laughter.

In the past there was a situation where a boy in a school had asked another pupil for sex. This is what it boiled down to, but the manner in which it was done was graphic. It was explained to the boy that he

275

could not under any circumstances behave like that. The boy apologised and said it would not happen again. The next time he encouraged a group of boys to surround the girl and ask for sex. The boy was eleven years old. Told again this was wrong did not deter him.

Later he physically abused the girl. When the situation was finally near a permanent exclusion from school the boy was supported by the parents saying he did not mean harm. This is true. He may not have meant harm but did the deed nevertheless. This is so hard to explain to the youngster. This is not love. It has nothing to do with love. It is rather giving in to the baser instinct of lust. We see the decline of moral teaching and we have increasing incidents like this in our society.

Sexually healed

Sexual healing is possible if you allow yourself to believe that love can be experienced between two people. Some survivors were surprised to discover that sex did not have to involve pain or any form of aggression. Sexual expression between two consenting adults that is shared cannot be bad. In our culture this is the last, and final, taboo, to talk about finding sexual expression after abuse or rape. In the illustrations in this chapter we are showing that consensual touch can lead toward healing.

There is a need to move beyond judgement and allow love between any consenting adults. Can you accept the challenge this chapter sets you to allow yourself to talk about sexual healing? You deserve to have a meaningful sex life.

Many survivors might experience problems with their sexual relationships at some point. Some might never manage to have fulfilling sex lives. Other survivors find that in the first months or few years in a relationship they are able to enjoy a sexual relationship with their partner. However, often following the birth of a child, or sometimes as a couple become more familiar with each other, they find that sexual touching or contact of any kind will trigger flashbacks and unpleasant memories associated with their previous traumatic experiences.

Although the experiences of sexual abuse or violence are totally different to the shared intimacy of a loving sexual relationship, there can be many reminders of abusive memories through touch and sensation, however well-meaning. This can be extremely difficult for partners who may feel that they are being seen as abusive themselves. They may feel hurt and rejected when their partner flinches away, or avoids contact with them.

Sexual healing begins with absolute trust between a couple. Both partners will have to accept that one or both of them are sensitive and vulnerable because of their past experiences.

Reflexology. This is an alternative therapy that you might consider as a way of pampering yourself. You should go to someone who is qualified. In reflexology they massage your feet. In the process they unlock the body's ability to heal itself. The basic philosophy is that the feet are a place that channel up to the whole body. Each part of the foot relates to another part of the body. Reflexology is not a solution to healing all on its own but is a useful aid. It can be called one of the alternative therapies for healing.

The healing journey

You might feel that you can never enjoy sex in the future. You may even feel there is a link with sexual abuse and sex. There is no connection between the two, but you may not know that sex does not have to be aggressive or unpleasant.

When you were abused your needs were not considered. You might think that sex is un-enjoyable. You might think you are inadequate and somehow damaged. You need to know that these things are not true and there is something you can do about it.

You need to know that sexual abuse is not sex. You need to find new associations for sex.

There are some significant trigger points that you may have noticed when problems with sex can happen:

> As your relationship moves to a more emotionally intimate level, when you start to feel more familiar with each other

> Following the birth of a child – either your own or to someone who is close to you

> When your own child or a child you know well reaches the same age as you were yourself when abuse started

> Following a high profile case in the news or on a TV programme involving rape or sexual abuse

When problems do happen, you might notice that sexual contact of any kind will trigger flashbacks and unpleasant memories associated with traumatic experiences. Sometimes, the fear of having a flashback is enough to put someone off wanting to have sex at all. Some survivors choose to remain celibate and never feel able to explore or accept their own responses and reactions to sexual intimacy.

Although the experience of sexual abuse or violence is totally different to the shared intimacy of a loving sexual relationship, touch, smell and sensation are powerful triggers to flashbacks. Partners may feel hurt and rejected when someone they love flinches away, or avoids contact with them.

FOUNDATIONS FOR SEXUAL HEALING

To begin to heal sexually, you will need to establish for yourself the basic foundations needed for this to happen:

- ➤ Safety – in the real world and in your own thoughts and feelings

- ➤ Trust – in yourself and your partner

- ➤ Reclaiming your body – being able to accept your body and how it responds and reacts to sensations

- ➤ Respect – your own and your partner's needs

- ➤ Communication – being able to express your needs and desires, and also being able to listen to your partner

- ➤ Triggers – identifying triggers and finding coping strategies for when flashbacks happen

- ➤ Joy and passion – developing new and joyful associations for sexual experiences

Safety – in the real world and in your own thoughts and feelings

'I want to be able to be aware of my feelings, I do not want to escape into unreality because of fear.' Amber

In any sexual activity you will need to feel safe and secure. You need to know that you are choosing to be involved in what is happening, that you will be treated with dignity and that your needs will be respected.

Create a safe place.

'Here in this beautiful room I have placed fresh flowers or pot pourri, candles that give a soft light and fragrance, incense to waft in the air, and soft cushions to lie on.

'I play soft, dreamlike music. When I smell the perfume, and see the space I have created, I feel delighted. I touch the beautiful fabric that is draped around me.

'All of these things help me control my imagination to create a wonderful atmosphere. There in that place I can feel confident to allow my partner to be intimate with me.

'I recommend that you try to do something like this for yourself. You can be as creative as you like.' Amber

Trust – in yourself and in your partner

'I want to be able to have enough trust with my partner that if at any point I want to say no, then they will stop.' Amber

'I want to be able to have sex and be involved emotionally.' Niles.

Take time for yourselves. You will have to explain to your partner that you need respect and deserve to be honoured. In order to be healed you will need to proceed in your own time. If at any point you feel that you cannot continue you can say stop. If you do not want to say stop then you could use another word. This could be negotiated with your partner. You need to choose a word that would be easier for you to say. It is like a code word that you and your partner agree upon.

> ➢ You will need to trust your partner
>
> ➢ Talk about possible boundaries
>
> ➢ Learn to trust your own intuition and thoughts
>
> ➢ You will need to build trust into the relationship before sex

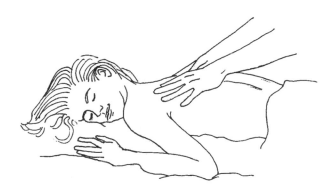

Reclaiming your body – being able to accept your body and how it responds and reacts to sensations

'I do not want to feel that my sex life has been stolen from me. I want to reclaim my body and my sex life.' Raoul.

➤ Give yourself permission to develop your feelings

➤ Allow yourself to react to physical sensations

➤ You will need to be comfortable in yourself

'I want to be able to explore my body and what arouses me.' Amber

➤ You need to enjoy being in your body. You might need to relearn how you feel inside your body. You do not want to feel physical or emotional pain

➤ You might have lots of tension that you will need to release. This needs to happen so that you can explore your feelings and enjoy the experience

 **Relaxation Exercise. Can be done on your own. You might try a breathing exercise that we have mentioned before. You might like to lie down and do some relaxation exercises. You might like to visualise yourself in a beautiful location swimming in a clear blue sea for example. Or you might like to harness special memories.**

'For a long time I felt embarrassed by my body. In a way I felt like it had let me down. In the end, I decided I had to change how I felt about myself. I started walking round the house naked, noticing how my body felt. When I felt comfortable, I stood naked in front of a mirror and looked carefully at myself. I realised that I am not disgusting or unattractive.' Amber

Respect – your own and your partner's needs

'I would like to fully enjoy my own body and sexuality and not have to ever be ashamed or justify myself to anyone.' Niles

> ➢ Talk to your partner about your needs

> ➢ You need to know that you are attractive to your partner

> ➢ You need to learn to ask for what you might enjoy

'I want to be loved for who I am.' Raoul.

Communication – being able to express your needs and desires, and also being able to listen to your partner

'I want to be the one to decide what I do sexually.' Amber

> ➢ You will need to talk to each other during sex

> ➢ You might like the opportunity to initiate sex

> ➢ You may need to relearn how to initiate sexual activity, especially if you have any confusion about asking for sex

> ➢ You can take the initiative by discovering what you enjoy and sharing that with your partner

> ➢ Give yourself permission to ask your partner for other things in your life. Then you will feel confident to ask for sexual pleasure

> ➢ Talk about your feelings

> ➢ Ask for a hug

> ➢ Hold eye contact and talk directly to them

> ➢ Write love poems to each other

> ➢ Exchange gifts of love

> ➢ Write scrolls of love tied with ribbons

> ➢ Massage each other

Triggers – identifying triggers and finding coping strategies for when flashbacks happen

'I want to be able to be happy in my body. I want to feel comfortable with being myself. I do not want to feel embarrassed by how feel in my own body.' Amber

Agree on a stop signal that will give you time to collect yourself, if you need to.

If during sexual activity you feel old memories and associations returning, you will need to talk to your partner about slowing down or stopping.

It is up to you if you would prefer to deal with the feelings after continuing with the sexual activity. You will want to be in the present reality and not back in an old abusive situation.

'I want my partner to be able to accept my sexual boundaries.' Amber

You may want to slow down and look around the room and focus on some of the beautiful things to remind yourself you are in the present and not in the past. You may want to stop.

You need to feel that you are in control. In time things should improve as you relearn how to enjoy your new experiences.

Joy and passion – developing new and joyful associations for sexual experiences

'I want to experience intimacy and love' Niles

- ➢ Building trust with intimacy
- ➢ Explore your comfort levels
- ➢ Hold each other
- ➢ You can give yourself permission to cry if you need to
- ➢ Just being in the presence of the one you love in this simple yet intimate way is itself an act of healing
- ➢ You might like to gently remove each other's clothes
- ➢ You might wish to approach sex like a ritual
- ➢ You both come to the space naked and prepared to sit opposite each other and slowly look into each others eyes
- ➢ Then slowly you may begin with the partner's permission to explore touching. This can be done in many imaginative ways. You have permission to explore your own sensuality

It is advised to go slowly. During this you are relearning new associations from anything you have experienced in the past. Breathe slowly and take your time.

 **Massage is a wonderful way of connecting with your own body and can be very simple and easy to do. When you are in the bath you can use bath oils to gently massage your arms and legs. Wooden massagers and sweet smelling oils can be used on hands and feet.**

Honouring your partner

'I was once told I was adorable. It made me feel valued; it was a moment of bliss, magic, utterly memorable. For the first time in my life I was cherished.' Niles.

It might be helpful to establish a ritual where you can show respect for each other, this applies to any relationship – heterosexual, gay or lesbian.

> ➤ You sit opposite each other and gaze lovingly into your partner's eyes
>
> ➤ Slowly massage one another's hands. This is a form of honouring the other person
>
> ➤ Then you can slowly progress in the touching to the whole body
>
> ➤ Then the touching can progress to more intimate areas

'Now that I have been through my sexual healing I can enjoy my own reactions to sexual activity without shame.' Niles

Sexual healing for survivors experiencing dissociative distress

If you experience dissociative distress or Dissociative Identity Disorder, then you will need to agree careful boundaries with your partner in the event that you dissociate or another identity emerges during lovemaking.

Your partner will need to know that this may happen and what will be the best way of responding. You will need to explain to your partner that you may dissociate or switch to a different identify during sexual activity.

This may not be easily noticed and you may not be aware yourself of what happens.

Your partner may notice:

➢ You may start to cry

➢ You may stop talking altogether

➢ You may stop moving

Your partner needs to know what they will need to do when they see this happening.

You may need to explain to your partner that if they ignore these signals and they continue the sexual activity then they are proceeding without your true consent. It may even be that the identity that emerges is a child personality who will experience any sexual activity as abusive.

What will help:

➢ Building complete trust with your partner so that you are confident that you will both respect each other's needs and wishes

The healing journey

➢ Agree on what will happen if your partner notices any of the above signs that you have dissociated or switched identity. You may need to stop any sexual activity at all, or you may need to alter what you are doing

➢ You need to know that you can regain control through developing excellent communication with your partner

Our message for people who are in for 'learning about love' stage of their healing journey:

> ➢ Be cautious and kind to yourself, relearning how to enjoy physical love. You have to learn new associations. For many, to regain a valuable sex life will take time. The key is a partner who will appreciate that at times you will be cautious and respect you for that. Past experiences may have created a template in your mind so that when someone touches or speaks to you in a certain way, flashbacks are triggered. It goes into the subconscious. It is a case of relearning how to experience things.

> ➢ Partners may be accustomed to sex being an activity that just happens rather than being thoughtful and planned. To appreciate each other should take time. The idea of partners gently learning how to literally honour one another and cherish each other can only be a good thing. Many books are on the market suggesting techniques for how to do this.

We also need to recognise that there are those who can never feel that they can have a successful sexual relationship with anyone. It is not helpful to tell everyone that they will find a partner, when this may not be so, and we all need to have the freedom to make personal choices without fearing judgement.

For some survivors, there may be lasting problems that will need to be directly addressed between the couple before they can resume their sexual relationship. Specialist sex therapy may be needed, and there are also books on reclaiming your sex life written specifically for survivors of sexual abuse.

We would encourage everyone who feels that they are not able to fully enjoy a sex life, to believe that this can be changed if this is what they want, and to seek out a sex therapist who can work with them to overcome the psychological barriers that still remain. Your GP may be able to refer you for therapy and The British Association for Counselling and Psychotherapy will be able to give you details of counsellors in your area who work with sexual difficulties.

What might help

Take the pressure off by agreeing with your partner that sexual intercourse or any sexual touching are out of bounds until you feel ready to move on to that stage. This might mean finding some self-help books specifically for survivors wishing to heal their sexual relationships.

Spend time as you start to work through the self-help books by slowly building trust between each other through shared activities – going out, walking, seeing films, and pampering each other.

If you feel you need specialist help, then your GP will be able to refer you on for psychosexual therapy.

Understand that partners may feel frustrated and disappointed even though they want to be supportive. They are struggling too.

> ➢ The only person who can heal the pain is YOU
> ➢ This is a surprise
> ➢ The restoration has to come from within
> ➢ You need to be able to celebrate who you are

CHAPTER 11

THE VISION

This final stage in the healing journey is our wish for all survivors. We hope that they will be able to use the words and suggestions to build for themselves the kind of future they want, where they can see themselves as healed from past trauma, effective in their everyday lives, and sharing love with the partner of their choice.

Not many people have ever thought about having a vision for themselves and you might think a vision is only for a certain type of person – maybe someone you imagine is successful and accomplished. Today, however we are offering you the chance to have a vision of your very own.

The vision

A vision is what you would like for yourself in the future. So think for a moment.

Above all you have a vision for yourself. That vision is to see yourself living a full and interesting life, aiming for those things that you feel you lost. Working towards a vision is a strong, motivational source of inspiration.

What sort of person would you like to be? We are not talking about a career here, like being a pilot, or an astronaut, or an estate agent. We are talking about you as an individual.

We know what many survivors' answers might be:

> 'I would like to just feel normal.'

> 'I want to feel happy again.'

But we want to inspire you to choose more than that.

What if your answer was 'I want to be:

- ➢ Successful
- ➢ Interesting
- ➢ To have influence
- ➢ To be respected
- ➢ To be dynamic
- ➢ To be motivated
- ➢ To be encouraging
- ➢ To feel fulfilled
- ➢ To feel wanted

 *Now is not the time to be timid. Get out a pen and put down some of the things you would really like to be!*

DYNAMIC

So many people imagine that they can never be dynamic. You might shy away from that thought. You may think being dynamic is for others and not for you. What would you be doing differently if you were being dynamic? How would you feel? What would you say? What does a confident and decisive person look like – what is their body language like?

You might want to be wonderful things, but can't imagine how to be great, happy, motivated and switched on! How do you become successful, amazing, sensational, marvellous, special and unique?

Well, guess what, you can choose what you want to be like. It is all a question of attitude. Your attitude determines everything you do or do not do. If you have a positive attitude toward your situation and your life, then things are going to go forward.

This seems obvious but it isn't. People have often come through bad times, but it is rare to meet someone who is going to tell you that you have to give yourself permission to be successful. So how about you simply give yourself permission to be what you would like to be? You deserve this for yourself after all. You have paid your dues.

Think about this question for a moment: What could you really do, if you put your mind to it?

Think about what you would like your relationships to be like. You can be a good friend, a supportive partner, a caring parent. You can be the work colleague who is thoughtful and sensitive to their workmates. You can be someone who donates time and energy to charities. These qualities cannot be bought, but are priceless.

AMAZING

You can be an amazing person if you try. You are already amazing. You have the qualities inside you that make you able to do amazing things. It is not wrong to want to be amazing. Do you know someone who is amazing? What do they do that you think is amazing? Perhaps there is something that you would like to do that could be amazing. If you set out to make or do something amazing for yourself, or someone else, then wow! It will be better than average, won't it? And here is the most amazing thing of all: You can and must be kind to yourself and give yourself permission to be amazing and successful.

Many survivors feel that they have lost out on career opportunities because of having to deal with the aftermath of abuse or rape. But, these days, there are many more opportunities to go back into adult education. Access courses allow students to start with the basics and work their way up to the course they wish to take.

Think about what you might need to learn for a particular career.

Can you learn something new? The answer is yes. However, you can only learn something if you are really motivated to learn it.

MEMORABLE

The world will be a really interesting place because you have lived in it. Do you believe that? You might say, 'If only that were true.' It could be true if you would like it to be. Consider what makes a person memorable. Is it their personality, their courage, their style, their commitment to a cause, or their personal values? For each person, this is different. To be remembered because you were able to give of your personality to others will be an important and significant step towards your own achievements.

Write down in what ways do you think you could be memorable?

_____

_____

_____

_____

_____

_____

_____

_____

_____

_____

This road to success is a journey you can start on now. What is important is what you decide you want that success to be. Remember the life-planning questions? What is important to you? What do you want to achieve? This is what your success will be built on.

You can also journey along the road to success by making progress towards your hopes and dreams. The most motivational factor of all is to have some hopes or dreams.

> ➢ If you have no vision for yourself you will never reach your goal
> ➢ If you tell yourself, 'I can't' then it won't happen

You can start building your own stepping-stones towards the vision you would like for yourself today. It all begins with commitment. Once you have a goal or dream then the want to achieve it follows.

PURPOSEFUL

It does help to have a purpose in living. Some have said that we exist to find our purpose in life. If we set out on our task with purpose, then it can help, rather than meandering aimlessly around in life.

We want to invite you all to come along the road to success. No one need be excluded. Anyone can be successful in their life. The main thing that matters is the confidence to do it.

If you walk into a room to meet someone and you smile, then people will respond positively. If you come into a room for an interview and you are withdrawn and boring then you will not get the job.

When we face the world with a smile, then more often than not it will be returned to us.

People make progress nowadays because they have confidence. 'Hold on', you might say, 'I do not do confident.' Then guess what? – If you act it you can feel it.

In the same way that your mood affects your body language, then your body language can affect your mood.

Think about what someone looks like when they're very down. They tend to move slowly, with their heads down, and with no interest in the world around them. They rarely smile or laugh, and their eye contact might be poor.

DELIGHTFUL

That person was delightful when I met them. You might say that of someone else but not yourself. What was it about them that made you think they were delightful? Was it their confidence? Their charm? Their humour? Do people consciously think they can be delightful? Maybe not consciously. What you can do is say, 'I am not going downward. I am building myself up to shine sometimes'. Then, hopefully, if you are working on your self-confidence, other things will fall into place and you will feel that you can be a delightful person.

When someone is feeling positive, then they have an energy in their movements, their heads are held up, and they take a keen interest in what's happening around them. They smile and make good eye contact when they meet someone.

The vision

We're not suggesting you can completely alter how you are behaving at the drop of a hat, especially if you're feeling low. We want you to have an awareness that how you are will have an impact on how others react to you.

MARVELLOUS

I will feel marvellous when I have found the ways to help me feel confident. I can then symbolically clothe myself with ideas and concepts that will raise my self-esteem. Then I will feel marvellous because I have achieved what I set out to do.

Can you think of someone who makes you feel happy or encouraged? What are the qualities they have that make you feel good? Are they caring, concerned, fun to be with, sympathetic, lively?

 *What can you do to develop positive qualities in yourself?*

_____

_____

_____

_____

_____

_____

Just by talking and showing you are not afraid, you will persuade people that you are confident. When you are going to meet new people, we suggest you think up some questions and topics for conversation beforehand.

People usually love talking about themselves and if you show interest in their answers, then they'll be very impressed with your communication skills.

In turn, they have the chance to show that they are interested in you. Yes, in you.

Guess what? PERSONALITY counts!

You may not have all the qualifications in the world. That does not matter. You may feel like you have been to hell and back. But, what matters more than anything is who you are - and that is where self - belief can change a person.

DISCOVERY

You can discover that inside you are a wonderful person. This is not easy but possible. Discover new ways of doing things. Discover new ideas you never thought you had. Discover a new you! You may discover that you have hidden talents!

You can be successful and you don't need to step on others' hopes along the way.

The vision represents all of these things:

Choices you are able to make

> ➢ Personal qualities - friendly, honest, enthusiastic, caring, responsible, respectful, trustworthy, fair

> ➢ What do you want your home to be like?

> ➢ What sort of atmosphere do you want in your home?

> ➢ Being and believing yourself to be a successful person

> ➢ Daring to dream for yourself

> ➢ Having the courage to have dreams for your future

> ➢ Believing in yourself

> ➢ Having a personal Vision for yourself and going after it

> ➢ Setting yourself goals

> ➢ Completing tasks

> ➢ Making progress

> ➢ Having an ambition

SENSATIONAL

Here we imagine someone running the marathon and smiling, thrilled at their achievement. We are all running a marathon. Along the way we have our children and our spouses or we are alone.

Despite how we are accompanied on our journey, we can say we have come this far. There has been damage, but there have been damage limitation exercises. This is no small feat. We have accomplished.

Hold the love you do have in your life as a precious gift.

Be strong and supportive of what is good in your life.

If there are issues that you have not confronted then know that you can confront them. Maybe not today, but one day.

Sensational is coming from a long way off and winning. I can succeed here despite the odds against me. Sensational is being a warm kind person, whose words offer encouragement to others despite what you have been through.

Dare to start liking yourself

If it is going to happen it must be up to me.

This simple teaching is very important:

If it is going to happen, it is going to be up to my attitude towards myself.

Here are some survivors' thoughts:

> 'I've never thought I could do anything worthwhile. I didn't even think I could be a good parent'

> 'I was the joker in the classroom. I made fun of myself before anyone else did. Never bothered with any work, and now it seems too late. I do wonder what I might have done with my life given the chance'

> 'I've made such a mess of my life. Everything always seems to have gone wrong. How can anything get better?'

CONFIDENCE

Confidence can be taught. In the theatre, actors learn confidence. It is an art. If you practice it you can get better. So many people think they can't be confident. They talk themselves out of being successful. Confidence can start with just one thought: 'I will try.' If you act confidently you can become confident. Consider how you talk and persuade somebody if you really want something. See, you can do it if you need to.

Self belief

If you do not believe in yourself, what is it you do not believe you could be, or achieve?

What is it that is stopping you from moving forward?

_____

_____

_____

_____

_____

_____

_____

_____

_____

_____

_____

This is the mental block that prevents you from going forward.

You have the privacy of knowing that the only person who will read this is you.

You are the only you in the entire history of the world, and you are only here once – make the most of yourself, you are unique

What are the things that make you the unique person you are and why?

What's your favourite food? Why?

_____

_____

_____

Favourite colour? Why?

_____

_____

_____

What music do you like? Why?

_____

_____

_____

What books do you read? Why?

_____

_____

_____

What is your favourite film? Why?

_____

_____

_____

What is your opinion about child abuse? Why?

_____

_____

_____

What is important to you? Why?

_____

_____

_____

What is important in society? Why?

_____

_____

_____

What are you interested in? Why?

_____

_____

_____

What do you like to do? Why?

_____

_____

_____

The vision

What would you do if you won a million pounds? Why?

What kind of people do you like? Why?

Are you a fun-loving extrovert? Why?

Are you a sensitive introvert? Why?

MAGNIFICENT

At times we have all felt insignificant and worthless. To be strong enough to be magnificent is an alien concept to many people. Here you have a task, to decide, if you want something to be successful you have to plan for it.

If you were going to create a magnificent makeover for a room and the client's brief was 'magnificent', what would you create? Magnificent is when you feel you can reach for the stars and be confident in yourself to stand up in a room and give a successful speech. When you know what you want and you aim for that because you say I deserve this. I have prepared. I have put in the time and the effort. I can have a chance.

We can't obviously be magnificent each day. Yet if you aim to ignite a spark in people's lives then it can be that occasionally you shine in yourself magnificently.

You will have to give yourself permission to be magnificent. Think of examples for yourself. Look at others. How was that person magnificent? Is there anything worth emulating in them? Is there a talent that you have that will help you to become magnificent?

Think ahead. I will need to be magnificent when I give a presentation at work in a few weeks' time. I will bake a magnificent cake for that birthday next week. I will wrap up that present magnificently with ribbons. In each of these cases a decision is being made, to aim towards being magnificent in some small but significant way.

If you build confidence slowly then you will allow yourself to be magnificent at least once in a while.

Your own Vision

This is your chance to write down what sort of vision you would like for yourself.

 *If you could dream up a reliable, realistic future for yourself, what would it be?*

_____

_____

_____

_____

_____

_____

_____

_____

_____

_____

_____

_____

_____

_____

_____

_____

AMBITION

You must have an ambition for yourself. This is not pride. To have an ambition is to have a goal to aim towards.

The first ambition that you do have is to take the first steps towards a better future.

To look at ambition differently and in more depth you should read Amber and Raoul's advice on a life plan.

The vision

 *Now, find quiet place and close your eyes for a few minutes. We want you to imagine yourself in your vision of the future.*

What do you look like in your Vision?

_____

_____

_____

What are you doing?

_____

_____

_____

What are you saying?

_____

_____

_____

What is happening?

_____

_____

_____

Imagine yourself in your chosen role. How do you feel?

_____

_____

_____

Is this something that you can put your hand on your heart and say, this is my true goal?

_____

_____

_____

What can you do today to start working towards your Vision?

_____

_____

_____

What short-term goals would you need in life, for yourself?

_____

_____

_____

In order to get to your Vision you need to start now!

DAZZLING

Could you dazzle someone with your personality and presence? If you combine all the confidence building with the new self- esteem armour that you have been working on, then hopefully you may feel you could dazzle others with your drive.

Most people are surprised to learn that, if you want something to happen, you have to make it happen.

 *If something is going to happen it will be up to my efforts. How does this statement help you?*

Where do we go from here?

If you want to achieve and be a success, then you have to strive towards that. Today, opportunities exist for everyone. Few realise this. They accept that the self-image they have is the one that will prevail.

It is not true that people who have been put upon cannot be successful. There have been many people who have had setbacks in the past. Oprah Winfrey was raped many times as a child, and yet overcame her distress to become emotionally and financially successful. You can do this as well. In David Peltzer's novel 'A child called It' he describes being abused by his mother and then going on to believe in himself and to write successful novels about self-help.

POTENTIAL

You have the potential to succeed. We know that we only use a small amount of our potential at times. There is so much value in our potential that we often ignore. Consider what potential you have within you to achieve your dreams.

The future

There is no one answer. There is a message. Life can be unfair. It seems more unfair to those who feel that it should not have happened in this way. It is important to remember that abuse never happens because of something the victim has done, but nothing can change the past.

However, we all have a future and the future is what we make it, starting right here and now in today. You may already have taken the step of wanting to have a better future. That is a positive act and you need to recognise it.

Many will be so hurt by their experiences that they feel their lives are ruined or that they are unable to make progress. For some people staying alive is in itself an act of courage, but they are surviving and coping in their own way. However, it is possible to move forward. A survivor is someone who can move forward.

Each step, however small, is one positive step towards a better future.

FLOURISH

'I feel as if I can go forward now having accepted some of the wisdom I have learned in my life. We all want to flourish not fail. Be aware that you flourish in having a calm mind, and not being agitated. When you make a good decision about yourself you are flourishing as a person, supported in self belief- and confidence.' Raoul

---

Our hope is that you will now feel you have your own Wizards of Inner Wisdom who can encourage you to achieve and consider yourself of value.

 We hope you might even want to buy yourself a Wizard or Teddy as a real reminder of your own positive and motivational messages. Make cards with all your positive words and statements, and keep them with your Teddy. Each day you can choose a word to inspire you.

In psychological terms it is you talking to and encouraging yourself.

Each day the positive words and messages reinforce their message of hope. You can even give yourself permission to be whatever you would like to be.

317

Spiritual

At this point some people will disagree with us including this concept. What has spirituality got to do with a book about sexual abuse? We do not want to get into a discussion about religion, yet one can't help but work from the culture and tradition you know and have been raised in.

'We believe that each person is a unique being – we are more than just flesh and bones. To harm a person's body is to harm their soul. We need healing in body, mind and soul. If there was an act that could heal a broken person from abuse, that could restore that person to lift their spirit up, and if we could find what this is, we would make it available to everyone.' Amber, Raoul & Niles.

'The spirit can be revitalised by being transfigured. We believe we can do this ourselves. Not everyone can imagine how hurt and destroyed a person can feel if they have been raped. How much lower can they go, if people say you are a lesser person for being abused?' Amber

'What if a person could say, 'I believe in my own spirit. Nothing can tear that out of me. I could restore my soul on my own, in myself. I wouldn't necessarily need potions or prayers.' Niles.

You could, if you feel confident enough, write your own creed and belief:

'I can find a sense of oneness and love from all creatures on earth. I can find harmony with nature in the countryside. I can feel the light of the sun on my face and fill my heart with the joy of being alive. I can ignite a joy in myself and a sense of self-motivation that will never diminish. I can stand up strong and say, 'I feel reborn. I can be restored to what I once was if I believe it. I can be pure of heart. I can set myself tasks and goals that will blaze a trail of glory. I can create. I can uplift. This comes from my spirit. The spirit I was born with. The heart that helps me feel the passion of my own convictions.' Niles

What is spirit? Is it the essence of a person? We each of us have an inner spark of life that is capable of growing and developing.

WRITE A LETTER TO YOURSELF!

Write a letter to yourself listing your accomplishments and achievements. You deserve to send that letter to your own address and thereby congratulate yourself on all that you have succeeded in.

**Keep making notes in your journal, on the progress
that you are making**

Here is a letter from a Survivor. It is included here as testimony for the need for healing. It is encouraging to know that there are many people who are on the same journey.

Dear Reader,

If you are reading this book, then you have been through abuse of some kind yourself or you are directly involved with a loved one who is. Well, this is a letter about me and what I went through and how the power of sharing and talking about my experience helped me through the hardest part of my life.

My abuse was perpetrated against me by an uncle and was kept a secret by me and my family for the best part of twenty years. I was six years old when the abuse began and it was started in a way where I did not have to 'perform' for my gifts. I am sorry if the word perform seems cold, but it is the only way I can describe the way the abuse was perpetrated.

My uncle would spoil me and he treated me like his best friend long before the abuse began. But, unfortunately, he was not my best friend. I was shown sexual pictures and asked if I was turned on by the experience, and then there was no stopping him. The sexual abuse started. If I did not do what he wanted, then he said I couldn't love him and he would pretend to cry.

This abuse, which included all but penetration, carried on until I was nine, every Sunday and every holiday.

My behaviour suffered and I was always in trouble in school and constantly ran away. This did not raise any alarms within the social services or at school. One particular day I was suffering constant physical abuse from my mother (yes, I was beaten by her regularly too) when I blurted out what was happening. The world stopped altogether, and then very slowly started moving again and then got faster and faster. My mother believed me at first, and then after a week she decided that her relationship with her brother and her own parents were more important to her than her relationship with me. I was told to apologise to my uncle for the 'evil lies' that I had told.

So, I buried the abuse, thinking that if I forgot about the abuse it would go away. My uncle had other ideas. The abuse started again, and he said that now we would be safe because everyone knew that I lied. The only time the abuse stopped was when, at the age of twelve, I asked my social worker to put me into care. That is when I started the long road to recovery.

I lived my life in control of my abuse experience quite well. It was buried. It did not affect me. Yeah, right. That is what I thought. If you ask the people who knew me, they would tell you a different story and now, on hindsight, so would I. I was an angry person, who exploded at the drop of a hat, and pushed away anyone who got near me. I destroyed my first girlfriend and fiancé, my friends and people who loved me, and I did not care. The breaking point came when I was throwing a bookcase across my son's room in temper, and saw the look of real fear in his eyes – I knew I needed help.

I went to my GP and he did not know what to do. I went to see a counsellor, and he panicked and said that I had done well by not wearing a dress and shooting people from a clock tower. Well, thanks, a lot!

At last the trail led to RoSA, a counselling service for anyone affected by rape or sexual abuse. I saw a counsellor for one-to-one sessions for a while, and then joined a male survivors' group, where there were other men who had been abused.

The feeling was fantastic. There were men there who had been abused, and they didn't have two heads and they were 'normal'. Wow! I felt electric, and so happy to be connected to the real world again and realise none of it was my fault.

With the help of counselling I have realised the power of talking and finding out about the effects of abuse on yourself and on the others around you.

If I could say anything to you reading this, it would be that the abuse is not, and never was your fault. No matter what you are told or what you think. The abuse was put on you and you don't own it, so stop saying 'my abuse' or 'my abuser'. Don't give them the power of owning you. Let them own the abuse they put on you. Be strong, be proud you survived and don't let the abuse destroy the great and beautiful person inside all of us.

With love from your fellow warrior.

Keiron Knights

Aged 32 and a survivor of sexual abuse

CHAPTER 12

HELPLINE AND WEBSITE CONTACT DETAILS

Specialist services

Directory and Book Services (DABS)
National Resource Directory, listing over
500 organisations in the UK and Ireland
offering services related to childhood abuse
and sexual abuse (£12)

www.dabsbooks.co.uk

DABS Resource Packs, including a list of
organisations in your own area, help sheets
(£3)

01709 860023

Counselling – finding a private counsellor

BACP (British Association for Counselling
and Psychotherapy)

0870 443 5252
www.bacp.co.uk

Counselling – finding a specialist service

DABSPathfinder Service - Counsellors
available to help you identify your need

01225 675351
www.dabspathfinder.org.uk

Alcohol Abuse

Drinkline Freefone

0800 917 8282

Helpline and website contact details

Children

Careline - Confidential Crisis telephone counselling service for children, young people and adults	020 8514 1177
Childline	0800 11 11
NSPCC Child Protection Helpline	0808 800 5000 www.nspcc.org.uk

Crisis helplines

Colchester Rape Crisis Line	01206 769795 www.crcl.org.uk
Rape and Sexual Abuse helpline	Men: 0808 800 0122 Women: 0808 800 0123
Samaritans	08457 90 90 90

Dissociative Distress

First Person Plural	www.firstperson.plural.org.uk

Domestic Violence

Women's Aid 24 hour National Helpline	08457 023468 www.womensaid.org.uk

Drug Abuse

Talk to Frank Freefone	0800 77 6600

Eating Disorders

Eating Disorders Association (EDA)	0845 634 1414 www.edauk.com

Events for Survivors

Survivors' March and Rally Against Child   020 8500 4914
Sexual Abuse

Survivors' Picnic in the Park   01788 551150

Incest - Support

CIS'ters (Childhood Incest Survivors)   023 8033 8080

Learning Difficulties

Respond   0808 808 0700
www.respond.org.uk

Voice UK   0870 013 3965
www.voiceuk.org.uk

Legal Issues - Support

Abuselaw   www.abuselaw.co.uk

ACAL (Association of Child Abuse   01923 286888
Lawyers)   www.childabuselawyers.com

Male Survivors

Survivors Swindon   0845 430 9371
www.survivorsswindon.com

Survivors UK   0845 122 1201
www.survivors.org.uk

Mental Health

Saneline   0845 767 8000
www.sane.org.uk

Helpline and website contact details

Threshold Women's Mental Health Infoline

0808 808 6000
www.thresholdwomen.org.uk

Young Minds

0800 018 2138
www.youngminds.org.uk

Parents

MOSAC Supporting non-abusing parents/carers

0800 980 1958
www.mosac.org.uk

Mothers of Abused Children

01697 331432

Parentline

0808 800 2222
www.parentlineplus.org.uk

Professionals – Abuse by

POPAN (Prevention of Professional Abuse Network)

0845 4500 300
www.popan.org.uk

Prevention of Child Sexual Abuse

NSPCC Child Protection 24 hr Helpline

0808 800 5000

NSPCC Child Protection Cymru/Wales

0808 100 25 24

Stop It Now!

0808 1000 900
www.stopitnow.org.uk

Ritual Abuse

01483 898600

RAINS (Ritual Abuse Information Network and Support)

01483 898600

Self-Injury

Bristol Crisis Service for Women

0117 925 1119
www.users.zetnet.co.uk

S.A.S.H. (Survivors of Abuse and Self Harm) Penfriend Network SAE for enquiries	20 Lackmore Road, Enfield, EN1 4PB

Sexual Assault Referral Centres

London – Haven – Camberwell	020 7347 1599/020 7737 4000
London – Haven – Paddington	020 7886 1101/020 7886 666
London – Haven – Whitechapel	020 7247 4787
Avon and Somerset – Milne Centre, Bristol	0117 928 3010
Kent – Renton Clinic, Dartford	01322 428 595
Derbyshire – Millfield House, Derby	01773 573840/1
Greater Manchester – St. Mary's Centre	0161 276 6515
Lancashire – Safe Centre, Preston	01772 523344
Leicestershire – Juniper Lodge, Leicester	0116 273 5461
Northumberland – Reach, Sunderland	0191 212 1551
Northumberland – Reach, Newcastle	0191 565 3725
West Midlands – Rowan Centre, Walsall	01922 644 329
Wiltshire – Swindon Sanctuary, Swindon	01793 709512

Websites

Phoenix Survivors	www.phoenixsurvivors.com
Safeline (for male and female survivors of child sexual abuse)	www.safelinewarwick.co.uk
AbuseLaw – legal issues and system in UK	www.abuselaw.co.uk

OTHER RESOURCES YOU MAY FIND HELPFUL

Books

Breaking Free	Carolyn Ainscough and Kay Toon
Partners in Healing	Teri Platt
The Courage to Heal Workbook	Laura Davis
The Self Harm Help Book	Lois Arnold and Anne Magill
The Sexual Healing Journey	Wendy Maltz
Victims No Longer	Mike Lew

Newsletters

Bristol Crisis Service for Women	PO Box 654, Bristol, BS99 1XH
CIS'ters (Childhood Incest Survivors)	PO Box 119, Eastleigh, SO50 9ZF
First Person Plural	PO Box 2537, Wolverhampton. WV4 4ZL
Respond	3rd Floor, 24-32 Stephenson Way, London. NW1 2HD
Survivors UK	2 Leathermarket Street, London. SE1 3HN